The Super Index To Windows Commands Plus

To order a copy of this book go to:

https://www.createspace.com/3666506

I DEDICATE THIS TO MY SON JAMES MY DAUGHTER TANNA AND MY GRANDCHILDREN WHO ARE THE LIGHT OF MY LIFE.

A VERY SPECIAL THANKS TO TWO SPECIAL PEOPLE THAT REALLY GREW CLOSE TO MY HEART WHO WAS THERE FOR ME THAT ENCOURAGED AND INSPIRED ME THAT GAVE ME MY SPACE AND TIME TO COMPLETE THE TASK.

MOST OF ALL I THANK GOD FOR THE INSPIRATION AND FOR THE KNOWLEDGE & RESOURCES HE HAS GIVEN ME TO WRITE THIS BOOK.

In Memory Of
Rochelle Scrivo
"Shell"

I WANT TO DEDICATE THIS BOOK TO MY NEICE THAT RECENTLY PASSED AWAY. SHE WILL BE GREATLY MISSED BY ALL OF US AND FOREVER REMEMBERED. SHELLY WE WILL ALL MISS YOU . WE WILL ALWAYS LOVE YOU.

Disclaimer

THIS IS NOT A COMPLEX BOOK BUT A QUICK REFERENCE GUIDE WITH BRIEF EXPLANATIONS, WITH ABOUT ALL THE WINDOWS COMMANDS YOU WILL EVER NEED.

EVER WISH YOU COULD HAVE ALL THE COMMANDS AT YOUR FINGERTIPS?

I SEARCHED EVERYWHERE FOR MONTHS FOR A BOOK LIKE THIS, NOT FINDING IT ANYWHERE. SURE THEY HAD COMPUTER TECH BOOKS. BUT WHAT THEY HAD WAS BOOKS WITH A LOT OF READING INVOLVED JUST TO GET TO WHAT I WANTED TO KNOW. PLUS WHEN I NEEDED TO GO BACK TO IT, IT WAS ALMOST IMPOSSIBLE TO FIND WITHOUT A LOT OF INTENSE READING.
THIS IS A PERFECT BOOK FOR THE BEGINNER OR EXPERT. NOT A LOT

OF GARBO, JUST PLAIN AND TO THE POINT WITH JUST BREIF EXPLANITIONS. WETHER YOUR GETTING A NEW TECH JOB OR ALREADY AN EXPERT AND KNOW MOST OF THE COMMANDS, THERE WILL BE NO SECOND GUESSING WHEN IT COMES TO WHICH COMMAND TO USE. ALSO INCLUDED IS REPAIR TECHNICS, BEEP CODES AND MANY MORE USEFUL TOOLS.

CONTENTS

WINDOWS & DOS
COMMANDS

YOU CAN RUN THESE FROM GOING TO START THEN RUN AND THEN TYPE THE COMMAND. THE COMMANDS THAT WON'T WORK THERE JUST TYPE CMD AND TYPE THEM AT THE COMMAND PROMPT. I'M NOT GOING TO GO INTO GREAT DETAIL ABOUT THESE COMMANDS, JUST A BREIF DESCRIPTION OF EACH. AFTER ALL I'M NOT TRYING TO FILL THIS BOOK FULL OF PAGES OF ENDLESS MATERIAL BUT A QUICK REFERENCE GUIDE THATS EASY TO ACCESS INFORMATION AT YOUR FINGERTIPS.

 WINDOWS XP ALSO HAS 40 OTHER SUPPORT TOOLS BESIDES THE TOOLS ALREADY INSTALLED WITH XP, THESE ARE ON THE WINDOWS CD., USED TO DIAGNOSE AND RESOLVE COMPUTER PROBLEMS.

COMMAND	DESCRIPTION	
A		FOR HELP WITH COMMANDS TYPE: Commandname ? AT THE COMMAND PROMPT.
arp	DISPLAYS AND CHANGES THE IP-TO-PHYSICAL ADDRESS USED TO MAP IP ADDRESS TO THE PHYSICAL MAC ADDRESSES.	

c:\users\toms pc>arp

Syntex: arp [options] {IP address} {MAC address} {Interface IP}

ARP

ADDRESS RESOLUTION PROTOCOL

-A   SHOWS THE CURRENT ARP DATA.

-G   SAME RESULTS AS -A.

-V   SHOWS THE INVALID DATA AND DATA
        ENTERED ON THE LOOP BACK INTERFACE.

ETH_ADDR   SHOWS A PHYSICAL ADDRESS.

INET_ADDR   SIGNIFIES AN INTERNET ADDRESS.

-N IF_ADDR   SHOWS ARP ENTRIES FOR THE
                PARTICULAR NETWORK INTER
                FACE IF_ADDR.

SHOWS THE VALUES ENTERED IN THE ARP CACHE TABLE. ALLOWS THE TABLES TO BE MODIFIED THAT STORE THE IP ADDRESSES AND THERE RESOLVED ETHERNET OR TOKEN RING ADDRESSES. THE TOKEN RING AND ETHERNET HAS THEIR OWN TABLE.

| assoc | DISPLAYS/CHANGE THE FILE NAME EXTENSIONS ASSOCIATIONS. TO DISPALY A LIST TYPE: ASSOC AT THE COMMAND PROMPT. |

COMMAND	DESCRIPTION
at	A SCHEDUALING UTILITY FOR PROGRAMS AND COMMANDS TO RUN AT A SPECIFIED DATE AND TIME ON THE SPECIFIED COMMPUTER. c:\users\toms pc>at ? at [\\hostcomputername] [id] [time] [options] ["commandname"] "COMMAND" — INDICATES THE COMMAND OR BATCH PROGRAM TO BE RUN. /DELETE — STOPS A SCHEDULED COMMAND FROM BEING RUN. ALL SCHEDULED COMMANDS ON THE MACHINE ARE CANCELED IF ID IS OMITTED. /EVERY:DATE[,...] — SETS THE COMMAND TO RUN ON THE DAYS SPECIFIED FOR THE WEEK OR MONTH. \\HOSTNAME — THE REMOTE COMPUTER THE COMMANDS ARE TO BE RUN ON. IF NO COMMAND IS GIVEN THEN IT RUNS ON THE LOCAL MACHINE. ID — SPECIFYS THE IDENTIFICATION NUMBER ASSIGNED TO A PARTICLAR SCHEDULED COMMAND. /INTERACTIVE — INTERACT'S THE JOB WITH THE DESKTOP OF THE CURRENT USER /NEXT:DATE[,...] — ALLOWS YOU TO SET THE SPECIFIED COMMAND TO THE NEXT EVENT OF THE DAY (EXAMPLE: NEXT FRIDAY). TIME — INDICATES WHAT TIME THE COMMAND IS GOING TO RUN. YES — ALL QUESTIONS WILL BE ANSWERED YES.

COMMAND	DESCRIPTION
atmadm	ATM ADMINISTRATOR MONITORS ADDRESSES AND CONNECTIONS REGISTERED BY THE ATM CALL MANAGER. TYPE: ATMADM TO MONITOR THE STATIS OF ACTIVE ATM CONNECTIONS. atmadm [options] -a FOR EACH ADAPTER THAT IS INSTALLED, THIS SHOWS THE NETWORK SERVICE ACCESS POINT FOR THE REGISTERED ATM. -c DISPLAYS ALL CALL INFORMATION FOR EVERY CONNECTION TO THE ATM ADAPTER. -s DISPLAYS INFO FOR THE ACTIVE ATM CONNECTIONS.
attrib	DISPLAYS/MODIFIES ATTRIBUTES FOR READ ONLY AND HIDDEN FILES AND DIRECTORIES. TYPE: ATTRIB TO DISPLAY ATTRIBUTES FOR THE CURRENT DIRECTORY. *c:\users\toms pc>attrib /?* *attrib [options...] [file]* + SETS THE ATTRIBUTE. - CLEARS THE ATTRIBUTE. a ARCHIVES THE FILE. h HIDES FILES. r READ-ONLY FILE. s SYSTEM FILES.
B	
batch	SCRIPTS OR PROGRAMS YOU CAN SCHEDULE TO RUN AUTOMATTLY AT SPECIFIED TIMES. BATCH FILES HAVE A .CMD OR .BAT EXTENSION TO THEM.

COMMAND	DESCRIPTION
bootcfg	THIS UTILITY ALLOWS YOU TO CHANGE, CONFIGURE OR QUERY YOUR BOOT.INI FILE, SUCH AS LOADING OPTIONS & SELECTING YOUR DEFAULT OPERATING SYSTEM. *c:\users\toms pc>bootcfg /?* *TYPE: bootcfg /copy /? REPLACE PARAMETER OPTION FOR COPY TO SEE THE HELP FILE FOR THAT PARTICLAR COMMAND* *bootcfg /parameter [arguments]* /? DISPLAYS HELP. /ADDSW ADDS PREDEFINED SWITCHES. /COPY COPIES AN EXISTING BOOT ENTRY. /DEBUG SETS PORT AND BAUD RATE FOR REMOTE DEBUGGING. /DELETE REMOVES EXISTING BOOT ENTRY OF THE BOOT.INI FILE. /DEBUG SETS PORT AND BAUD RATE FOR REMOTE DEBUGGING. /DEFAULT CHANGES DEFAULT BOOT ENTRY. /DBG1394 CONFIGURES 1394 PORT FOR DEBUGGING. /QUERY SHOWS CURRENT BOOT ENTRIES AND SETTINGS.
break	USED ONLY FOR CAPATIBILITY ISSUES WITH MS-DOS FILES.
C	
cacls	MODIFIES AND DISPLAYS THE DISCRETIONARY ACCESS CONTROL LIST (DACL)

COMMAND	DESCRIPTION
calc	*WINDOWS* CALCULATOR
call	USE TO CALL ONE BATCH PROGRAM FROM ANOTHER WITHOUT INTERFERRING WITH THE PARENT BATCH PROGRAM. THIS COMMAND HAS WILL NOT WORK AT THE COMMAND-LINE IF USED OUTSIDE OF THE SCRIPT OR BATCH FILE.
change	USED WITH TERMINAL SERVICES TO CHANGE COMMANDS.
chcp	SHOWS THE NUMBER FOR THE ACTIVE CONSOLE CODE PAGE.
chdir or cd	CHANGE'S THE DIRECTORY (EXAMPLE IF IN A:\ DIRECTORY AND CHDIR C:\ IS TYPED IT CHANGES THE DIRECTORY FROM THE A:\ DIRECTORY TO THE C:\ DIRECTORY.)

COMMAND	DESCRIPTION
chkdsk	CHECK DISK CHECKS THE DISK FOR ERROR'S THEN GIVES YOU THE OPTION TO CORRECT THE ERRORS FOUND. c:\users\me>chkdsk /? chkdsk [drive] [path] [filename] [options...] /F USE TO FIX ERRORS ON THE DISK. /I CARRIES OUT A LESS DYNAMIC CHECK OF INDEXED DATA FOR NTFS ONLY. /R RECOVERS ALL READABLE INFORMATION AND LOCATES BAD SECTORS. /V USE TO SHOW THE NAME AND PATH OF ALL THE FAT AND FAT32 FILES ON THE DISK. /X FORCES VOLUME DISMOUNT IF NECESSARY.
chkntfs	NTFS FILE SYSTEM CHECK.
cipher	ENCRYPTS OR DECRYPTS FILES.
clipbrd	CLIPBOOK VIEWER.
cls	CLEARS THE SCREEN.
cmd	STARTS THE COMMAND INTERPRETER.
cmstp	INSTALLS AND REMOVES THE CONNECTION MANAGER SERVICE PROFILE.

COMMAND	DESCRIPTION
color	CHANGES THE COLOR FOR THE COMMAND PROMPT WINDOW FORGRAUND AND BACK-GROUND COLORS.
command	OPENS COMMAND INTERPRETER.
comp	COMPARES CONTENTS OF FILES BYTE BY BYTE ON THE SAME DRIVE OR ON DIFFERENT DRIVES OR DIRECTORIES. c:\users\toms pc>comp /? FOR FILE1 AND FILE2 USE WILD CARDS TO COMPARE SETS OF FILES. comp [file1] [file2] [options...] /D SHOWS THE DIFFERENCES IN DECIMAL FORMAT. /A PUTS ON DIFFERENCES ON VIEW IN ASCII CHARACTERS. /L SHOWS THE LINE NUMBERS FOR THE DIFFERENCES. /N DOES A COMPARISON OF ONLY THE FIRST NUMBER OF LINES SPECIFIED FOR EACH FILE FILE1 POINTS OUT THE NAME AND LOCATION OF THE FIRST SET OF FILES TO COMPARE. FILE2 POINTS OUT THE NAME AND LOCATION OF THE SECOND SET OF FILES TO COMPARE.
compact	COMPRESSES FILES AND DISPLAYS THE STATE OF THE DIRECTORY ON NTFS PARTITIONS.
convert	CONVERTS FAT FILE VOLUMES TO NTFS.

COMMAND	DESCRIPTION
control	OPENS CONTROL PANEL APPLETS. (TO LAUNCH ADMIN UTILITY TYPE: CONTROL USERPASS-WORDS2).
copy	COPIES FILES FROM ONE LOCATION TO AN-OTHER.
Ctrl + Alt + Del	DISPLAYS TASK MANAGER. PRESS THE SE-QUENCE THREE TIMES TO REBOOT.
D	
date	SHOWS THE DATE OF THE SYSTEM AND PROMPTS FOR A NEW DATE. SYNTAX: date [mm-dd-yy] MM — SELECT TWO DIGITS FOR THE MONTH. DD — SELECT TWO DIGITS FOR THE DAY. YY — SELECT TWO DIGITS FOR THE YEAR. DATE /T — DISPLAYS THE CURRENT DATE WITH OUT CHANGING IT.
debug	USED TO TEST AND DEBUG *MS-DOS* EXECUT-ABLE FILES.
defrag	DEFRAGMENTS THE DRIVE, BRINGS THE FRAG-MENTED FILES TOGETHER.

COMMAND	DESCRIPTION
del	DELETES THE FILES SPECIFIED.
dir	SHOWS A LIST OF DIRECTORIES AND SUBDIRECTORIES.
diskcomp	COMPARES CONTENTS OF TWO FLOPPY DISK. WHEN USED WITHOUT PARAMETERS IT USES THE CURRENT DRIVE FOR BOTH DISK.
diskcopy	COPIES THE CONTENTS OF ONE FLOPPY DISK ONTO ANOTHER.
diskpart	TEXT VERSION OF THE GUI DISK MANAGER TO MANAGE YOUR DISK PARTITIONS.
doskey	RECALL COMMANDS, EDITS COMMAND LINES, AND CREATES MACROS.

COMMAND	DESCRIPTION
driver query	DISPLAYS A LIST OF DRIVERS AND THEIR PROPERTIES. c:\users\toms pc>driverquery /? driverquery [options...] /? HELP, BRINGS UP A LIST OF PARAMETERS TO USE. /FO FORMAT INDICATES WHAT TYPE OF OUTPUT TO FETCH. /P [PASSWORD] INDICATES THE PASSWORD FOR THE GIVEN USER. /S SYSTEM IDENTIFIES THE REMOTE SYSTEM TO WHICH YOU WILL CONNECT TO.
drwtsn32	TOOL USED TO DEBUG AND SHOWS LOGS FOR ANY ERRORS FOUND.
E	
echo	DISPLAYS THE ECHO SETTINGS WHEN ECHO IS TURNED ON.
edit	TEXT FILE EDITOR.

COMMAND	DESCRIPTION
endlocal	THIS COMMAND ENDS THE LOCAL SETTINGS OF THE ENVIRONMENTIAL CHANGES IN A BATCH FILE. RETURNS THE ENVIRONMENTAL VALUES BACK TO THE VALUES THEY HAD BEFORE USING THE SETLOCAL COMMAND.
erase	DELETES FILES.
eudcedit	PRIVATE CHARACTER EDITOR BUILT INTO THE *WINDOWS* THAT YOU CAN CREATE YOUR OWN FONT.
eventcre-ate	ALLOWS THE ADMINASTRATOR TO ADD A MES-SAGE TO THE EVENTS LOG.
event-query	DISPLAYS A LIST OF EVENTS FROM THE EVENT LOGS.
eventtrig-gers	DISPLAYS AND CONFIGURERS THE EVENT TRIGGERS FOR BOTH LOCAL AND REMOTE MACHINES.
exit	EXITS THE CURRENT COMMAND OR BATCH SCRIPTS.
expand	USED TO RETRIEVE COMPRESSED FILES FROM DISTRIBUTION DISK.
explorer	OPENS A NEW EXPLORER WINDOW.
F	

COMMAND	DESCRIPTION
fc	COMPARE THEN DISPLAYS THE DIFFERENCES BETWEEN TWO FILES.
filter commands	SORT, VIEW, AND SELECT SPECIFIED SECTIONS OF A COMMAND OUTPUT.
find	SEARCHES FOR THE TEXT STRING SPECIFIED AND DISPLAYS IT.
findstr	SEARCHES FOR STRING PATTERNS AND DISPLAYS THEM.
finger	DISPLAYS INFORMATION ABOUT ONE OR MORE USERS ON A REMOTER COMPUTER. WITHOUT PARAMETERS IT SHOWS THE HELP MENU.
flattemp	ENABLES OR DISABLES TEMPORY FLAT FOLDERS.
fontview	DISPLAYS THE SPECIFICED FONT.
for	RUNS THE COMMAND SPECIFIED FOR EVERY FILE IN A SET OF FILES.

COMMAND	DESCRIPTION
format	FORMATS THE DISK SPECIFIED.
fsutil	USED TO MANAGE REPARSE POINTS, MANAGING SPARSE FILES, DISMOUNTING A VOLUME, OR EXTENDING A VOLUME. MUST BE LOGGED IN AS A ADMINSITRATOR.
ftp	FILE TRANSFER PROTOCOL FOR TRANSFERING FILES TO AND FROM A COMPUTER.
ftype	SHOWS OR MODIFYS FILE TYPES USED IN THE FILE EXTENTSION ASSOCIATIONS.
G	

COMMAND	DESCRIPTION
getmac	DISPLAYS THE MEDIA ACCESS CONTROL (MAC) ADDRESS FOR EACH NETWORK ADAPTERS ON YOUR MACHINE. c:\users\toms pc>getmac PHYSICAL MAC ADDRESS TRANSPORT NAME 00-9E-15-A4-F8-B0 MEDIA DISCONNECTED 00-22-C2-27-11-AD MEDIA DISCONNECTED c:\users\toms pc>getmac /? getmac [options...] /? DISPLAYS THIS HELP MESSAGE. /P [PASSWORD] SETS THE PASSWORD GIVEN FROM THE USER. /S SYSTEM IDENTIFIES THE REMOTE SYSTEM TO CONNECT TO. /U [DOMAIN\]USER SELECTS THE USER ENVIRONMENT THE COMMAND SHOULD IMPLEMENT. /V SPECIFIES THAT VERBOSE OUTPUT IS DISPLAYED.
goto	USED WITHIN PROGRAM SCRIPTS TO CONTROL FLOW.
gpresult	DISPLAYS A SUMMARY OF USER AND GROUP POLICY SETTINGS.
gpupdate	A UTILITY FOR APPLYING COMPUTER AND USER POLICYS.

COMMAND	DESCRIPTION
graftabl	ALLOWS YOU TO DISPLAY THE EXTENDED CHARACTER SET IN GRAPHICS MODE.
H	
help	DISPLAYS A LIST OF EVERY SYSTEM COMMAND AND BRIEF DESCRIPTION OF EACH.
helctr	DISPLAYS HELP AND SUPPORT CENTER HOME PAGE AND USING PARAMETERS DISPLAYS THE HELP AND SUPPORT CENTER.
hostname	DISPLAYS THE HOSTNAME.
hypertrm	USED TO CONNECT TO OTHER COMPUTERS, INTERNET TELNET, BULLETIN BOARDS AND MORE.
I	
if	USED IN BATCH PROGRAMS TO CONDITIONALLY PERFORM A COMMAND.
ipconfig	DISPLAYS AND CONFIGURES THE IP ADDRESS, SUBNET MASK, AND DEFAULT GATEWAY FOR ALL ADAPTERS.
ipseccmd	CONFIGURES THE INTERNET PROTOCOL SECURITY (IPSEC) POLICIES IN A LOCAL OR REMOTE REGISTRY.
ipxroute	DISPLAYS THE SETTINGS FOR PACKETS SENT TO UNKNOWN, BROADCAST, AND MULTICAST ADDRESSES.

COMMAND	DESCRIPTION
irftp	IRFTP (INFRARED FTP) USED TO SEND FILES VIA INFRARED. OPENS THE WIRELESS DIALOG BOX TO SELECT FILES TO SEND.
L	
label	USED TO CHANGE OR DELETE THE CURRENT VOLUME LABLE.
logman	USED TO MANAGE THE PERFORMANCE MONITOR.
lpq	DISPLAYS THE PRINTER QUEUE STATUS.
lpr	DISPLAYS HELP FOR THE LPR COMMAND.
M	
mkdir or md	CREATES A NEW DIRECTORY OR SUBDIRECTORY.
mmc	*MICROSOFT* MANAGEMENT CONSOLE.
mode	ALLOWS YOU TO CONFIGURE A SYSTEM DEVICE.
more	DISPLAYS THE OUTPUT ON THE MACHINE ONE SCREEN AT A TIME.

COMMAND	DESCRIPTION
mountvol	MANAGES, CREATES, LIST AND DELETES A VOLUME MOUNT POINT. c:\users\toms pc>mountvol /? Syntax: mountvol [drive] [path] [volume] [options...] /? — DISPLAYS THIS HELP MESSAGE. /P [PASSWORD] — SETS THE PASSWORD GIVEN FROM THE USER. /S SYSTEM — IDENTIFIES THE REMOTE SYSTEM TO CONNECT TO. /U [DOMAIN\]USER — SELECTS THE USER ENVIRONMENT THE COMMAND SHOULD IMPLEMENT. /V — SPECIFIES THAT VERBOSE OUTPUT IS DISPLAYED.
move	ALLOWS YOU TO MOVE FILES FROM ONE FOLDER TO ANOTHER.
msconfig	TO CHANGE THE START-UP SERVICES AND UTILITIES THAT LOAD ON BOOT UP.
msiexec	*MICROSOFT WINDOWS* INSTALLER ALLOWS YOU TO INSTALL, MODIFY AND PERFORM OPERATIONS FROM THE COMMAND-LINE ON INSTALL

COMMAND	DESCRIPTION
msinfo32	DISPLAYS THE SOFTWARE ENVIRNMENT ALONG WITH A VIEW OF THE HARDWARE AND SYSTEM COMPONENTS.
N	
narrator	STARTS UP THE SYSTEM NARRATOR.
nbtstat	DISPLAYS THE CURRENT TCP/IP CONNECTIONS USING NETBIOS OVER TCP/IP AND PROTOCOL INFORMATION. c:\users\toms pc>nbtstat nbtstat [options…] [interval] -a DISPLAYS THE REMOTE COM PUTER'S NAME TABLE BY ITS NAME. -A DISPLAYS THE REMOTE COMPUTER'S NAME TABLE BY ITS IP ADDRESS. -c DISPLAYS THE NETBIOS CACHE NAME AND IP ADDRESS ON THE REMOTE COMPUTER. -n DISPLAYS A LISTS OF LOCAL NETBIOS NAMES. -r DISPLAYS A LISTS OF NAMES RESOLVED BY BROADCAST AND VIA WINS -R PURGES ALL NAMES FROM THE NETBIOS NAME CACHE AND THEN RELOADS THE REMOTE CACHE NAME TABLE -S DISPLAYS THE SESSIONS TABLE ALONG WITH THE DESTINATION IP ADDRESSES -s DISPLAYS THE SESSIONS TABLE AND CHANGES THE REMOTE DESTINATION IP ADDRESSES TO NETBIOS NAMES USING THE HOST FILE. -RR REFRESHES AFTER SENDING NAME RELEASE PACKETS TO WINS. INTERVAL KEEPS DISPLAYING THE INFORMATION WHILE PAUSING SPECIFIED INTERVAL SECONDS BETWEEN

COMMAND	DESCRIPTION
netsh	NETWORK CONFIGURATION TOOLS USED TO CONFIGURE NETWORK INTERFACES, *WINDOWS* FIREWALL AND REMOTE ACCESS. ALLOWS YOU TO LOCALLY OR REMOTELY DISPLAY OR MODIFY NETWORK CONFIGURATION. TYPE: NETSH AT THE COMMAND PROMPT. AFTER NETSH> TYPE ? TO LEARN MORE ABOUT THIS UTILITY.

c:\users\toms pc>netsh /?

SYNTAX: netsh [options…] [command]

?	SHOWS INFORMATION FOR COMMANDS AVAILABLE. TYPE: COMMAND ?
ADD	ADDS AND CONFIGURES AN ENTRY TO A LIST OF ENTRIES.
ADVFIREWALL	USED TO MAKE CHANGES TO NETSH ADVFIREWLL.
BRIDGE	ALLOWS YOU TO CHANGE TO THE NETSH BRIDGE ENVIRONMENT.
DELETE	DELETES CONFIGURATION SETTINGS FROM A LIST OF DATA EN TRIES.
DHCPCLIENT	CHANGES TO THE NETSH DHCPCLIENT ENVIRONMENT.
DUMP	LOGS AND DISPLAYS TO A CONFIGURATION SCRIPT.
EXEC	RUNS A SCRIPT FILE OF COMMANDS TO BE EXECUTED.
FIREWALL	CHANGES OVER TO THE `NETSH FIREWALL' ENVIRONMENT.
HELP	SHOWS THE COMMANDS TO BE USED WITH NETSH.
HTTP	CHANGES THE ENVIRONMENT TO NETSH HTTP.INTERFACE

COMMAND	DESCRIPTION

netstat	DISPLAYS A LIST OF ALL ACTIVE TCP/IP NETWORK CONNECTIONS AND PROTOCOL STATISTICS.
	
	c:\users\toms pc>netstat /?
	netstat [options…] [interval]
	
	   -A BRINGS UP A LIST OF ALL CONNECTIONS AND LISTENING PORTS.
	   -E MAY BE COMBINED WITH THE -S OPTION TO SHOW ETHERNET STATISTICS.
	   -F BRINGS UP AND DISPLAYS THE FULLY QUALIFIED DOMAIN NAMES (FQDN) FOR FOREIGN ADDRESSES.
	   -N SHOWS THE PORT NUMBERS AND ADDRESSES IN NUMERICAL FORM.
	   -O SHOWS THE OWNING PROCESS ID LINKED WITH EACH CONNECTION.
	   -R SHOWS THE ROUTING TABLE ON THE DISPLAY.

nslookup	NAME RESOLUTION TOOL USED TO DISPLAY INFORMATION FROM DOMAIN NAME SYSTEM (DNS) NAME SERVERS.
ntbackup	USED TO BACKUP FOLDERS TO TAPE.
ntsd	THIS COMMAND WAS ADDED FOR USE BY SOFTWARE DEVELOPERS ONLY.
net	USED TO MANAGE NETWORK RESOURCES.
O	

COMMAND	DESCRIPTION
openfiles	QUIRIES, DISPLAYS OR DISCONNECTS OPEN FILES USED BY NETWORK USERS. FOR ADMINISTORS.
P	
pagefile-config	DISPLAYS AND CONFIGURES THE PAGING FILE VIRTUAL MEMORY SETTINGS OF A SYSTEM. FOR ADMINISTORS.
path	DISPLAYS THE CURRENT COMMAND PATH.
pathping	A MIXTURE OF TRACEROUTE AND PING UTILITIES. USED TO DETERMINE WHICH ROUTER OR SUBNETS IS HAVING A NETWORK PROBLEM.
pause	USED IN BATCH SCRIPTS TO STOP THE PROCESSING OF A BATCH PROGRAM. PROMPTS USER FOR ACTION TO CONTINUE.
pbadmin	PHONE BOOKS FOR ADMINISTORS.
pentnt	PENTIUM CHIP FLOATING POINT DIVISION ERROR DETECTION. DISABLES THE HARDWARE AND TURNS ON EMULATION.
perfmon	PERFORMANCE MONITOR
ping	ALLOWS YOU TO TEST A NETWORK CONNECTION FOR NETWORKED COMPUTERS, ROUTERS, OR INTERNET SITES.
popd	RESTORES THE CURRENT DIRECTORY TO THE DIRECTORY STORED BY THE PUSHD COMMAND.

COMMAND	DESCRIPTION
print	PRINTS DISPLAYED ITEM TO A PRINTER.
prncnfg	DISPLAYS CONFIGURATION INFORMATION OR CONFIGURES A PRINTER.
prndrvr	RETURNS A LIST OF PRINTER DRIVERS. ADD OR DELETE A PRINTER DRIVER.
prnjobs	RETURNS A LIST OF PRINT JOBS. ALLOWS YOU TO PAUSE, CANCEL, AND RESUME A PRINT JOB.
prnmngr	RETRIEVES A LIST OF PRINTERS AND PRINTER CONNECTIONS. ALLOWS YOU TO ADD OR DELETE A PRINTER OR PRINTER CONNECTION.
prnport	ALLOWS YOU TO CHANGE PRINTER PORT CONFIGURATIONS AND CREATES, DELETES, AND LIST STANDARD TCP/IP PRINTER PORTS.
prnqctl	PAUSES AND RESUMES A PRINTER JOB. ALLOWS YOU TO PRINT A TEST PAGE, CLEARS THE QUEUE.
prompt	ALLOWS YOU TO CHANGE THE PROMPT.
powercfg	MANAGES POWER SETTINGS.

COMMAND	DESCRIPTION
pushd	THIS WILL SAVE THEN STORE THE NAME OF THE CURRENT DIRECTORY AND THEN CHANGES THE NAME TO A SPECIFIED NAME FOR THE CURRENT DIRECTORY.
R	
rasdial	MANAGES THE RAS CONNECTIONS AND DISPLAYS THE STATUS OF ANY CONNECTIONS.
rcp	WITH THE RSHD RUNNING ON THE NON XP COMPUTER THIS COMMAND COPIES THE FILES FROM ONE COMPUTER TO ANOTHER. *WINDOWS* AND WIN 2000 DOES NOT PROVIDE THE RSHD SERVICE.
recover	ATTEMPTS TO RECOVER READABLE DATA FROM A DISK THAT HAS BAD OR DEFECTIVE FILES.
reg	REGISTRY VALUES AND SUBKEY INFORMATION. ALLOWS YOU TO ADD, CHANGE OR DELETE REGISTRY ENTRIES.
regsvr32	REGISTERS OR UNREGISTERS .DLL FILES IN THE REGISTRY AS COMMAND COMPONENTS.

COMMAND	DESCRIPTION
relog	CREATES A LOG FILE INTO READABLE CONTENT SUCH AS A TEXT LOG FILE AN OTHER FORMATS, EXTRACTS PERFORMANCE COUNTERS FROM PERFORMANCE COUNTER LOG FILES.
rem	ADD COMMENTS TO CONFIG.SYS OR IN A BATCH FILE.
rename or ren	RENAME FILES OR A SET OF FILES.
replace	ALLOWS YOU TO UPDATE OR REPLACE FILES IN THE DESTINATION DIRECTORY WITH FILES IN THE SOURCE DIRECTORY WITH THE SAME NAME.
reset session	DELETE A SESSION FROM TERMINAL SERVER.
rexec	AUTHENTICATES USERNAME ON REMOTE MACHINE BEFORE IT EXECUTES THE SPECIFIED COMMAND TO RUN.

COMMAND	DESCRIPTION
rmdir or rd	Removes directory.
route	Used to mnipulte entries in local ip network routing table then displays the information.
rsh	To run commands on a remote computer, the remote computer must be running the rsh service. *Windows* does not support the rsh service.
rsm	Allows you to run batch scripts for applications that don't support removable storage api. used to manage media resources that are using removable storage.
runas	Executes programs and tools using a different user account.
S	
sc	Service controller is used to make changes to the services dealing with logon, logoff, startup, or shutdown scripts.
schtasks	Schedules programs or commands at a specified time on a local or remote computer. Allows you to add, remove, start or stop task then displays the changes made to scheduled tasks.

COMMAND	DESCRIPTION
secedit	USE TO MANUALLY SET COMPUTER AND USER POLICYS. THIS UTILITY ANALYZES THE SYSTEM SECURITY THEN CONFIGURES THE SYSTEM BY COMPARING YOUR SYSTEMS CURRENT CONFIGURATION.
set	USED TO REMOVE, SET AND DISPLAY ENVIRONMENTAL VARIABLES.
setlocal	USED TO CONTROL ENVIRONMENTAL VISIBILITY OF VARIABLES.
sfc	SYSTEM FILE CHECKER SCANS SYSTEM FILES / APPLICATIONS AND REPLACES THE CORRUPTED FILES WITH OFFICIAL MICROSOFT VERSIONS.
shift	WORKS WITH BATCH FILES BY CHANGING THE POSITIONING OF THE BATCH PARAMETERS.
shutdown	USED TO SHUTDOWN OR RESTART THE COMPUTER LOCALLY OR REMOTE.
sigverif	VERIFIES THE DRIVER IS MICROSOFT APPROVED.

COMMAND	DESCRIPTION
sort	READS, SORTS, AND WRITES DATA AND DISPLAYS RESULTS TO FILE OR ANOTHER DEVICE.
start	OPENS A NEW COMMAND WINDOW AND STARTS AN APPLICATION.
subst	LINKS A PATH TO A DRIVE LETTER. USED WITHOUT PARAMETERS, DISPLAYS THE CURRENT VIRTUAL DRIVES.
system-info	DISPLAYS SYSTEM CONFIGURATION INFORMATION WHICH INCLUDES THE OPERATING SYSTEM, SECURITY INFORMATION, HARDWARE PROPERTIES, RAM, NETWORK CARDS, DISKSPACE, AND PRODUCT ID .
sysedit	SYSTEM CONFIGURATION UTILITY EDITOR. MSCONFIG IS WHAT IS USED NOW.
T	
taskkill	STOPS ONE OR MORE TASK OR PROCESS THAT IS LOCKED UP OR RUNNING. CAN BE STOPPED BY IMAGE NAME OR PROCESS ID.
tasklist	DISPLAYS THE SERVICES AND RUNNING APPLICATIONS FOR ALL TASK ALONG WITH THEIR PROCESS ID (PID) ON THE LOCAL OR REMOTE COMPUTER. A MUST HAVE FOR FIGHTING VIRUSES.

COMMAND	DESCRIPTION
tcmsetup	A TOOL FOR THE TAPI CLIENT THAT ALLOWS YOU TO SET UP OR DISABLE THE TAPI CLIENT.
tftp	TO BE USED WITH REMOTE COMPUTERS TO TRANSFER FILES TO AND FROM.
time	DISPLAYS THE SYSTEM TIME.
title	USED WITH THE COMMAND PROMPT WINDOW TO SET A TITLE FOR A CMD.EXE SESSION.
tracerpt	DISPLAYS TRACE LOGS IN REAL-TIME DATA FROM TRACE PROVIDERS ALSO ALLOWS YOU TO GENERATE TRACE ANALYSIS REPORTS AND CSV FOR EVENTS GENERATED.
tracert	TRACE'S THE PATH TAKEN TO THE DESTINATION OF A REMOTE HOST WITH TIME TO LIVE (TTL) VALUES.
tree	A TREE STYLE DISPLAY FOR THE FOLDER OR DRIVE SPECIFIED.
type	DISPLAYS THE TEXT FILE CONTENTS.

COMMAND	DESCRIPTION
typeperf	WRITES THE PERFORMANCE COUNTER DATA TO A LOG FILE OR A COMMAND WINDOW. TYPE: TYPEPERF TO STOP THEN CTRL+C.
U	
unlodctr	THIS WILL ALLOW YOU TO REMOVE THE NAME FROM THE PERFORMANCE COUNTER AND FROM THE REGISTRY.
V	
ver	THIS WILL DISPLAYS THE *WINDOWS* VERSION INFORMATION.
verify	USED IN *WINDOWS* WITH MS-DOS FILES FOR COMPATIBILITY.
vol	DISPLAYS THE VOLUME LABEL FOR THE DISK AND SERIAL NUMBER.

COMMAND	DESCRIPTION
vssadmin	VOLUME SHADOW COPY SERVICE ADMINISTRATIVE COMMAND-LINE TOOL THAT LIST PROVIDERS, SHADOWS, SHADOW STORAGE, VOLUMES, WRITERS, AND RESIZES SHADOW STORAGE.
W	
w32tm	DIAGNOSTIC TOOL USED TO CORRECT PROBLEMS WITH *WINDOWS* TIME.
winnt	INSTALLS OR UPGRADES TO *WINDOWS*.
winver	DISPLAYS THE *WINDOWS* VERSION.

THESE FTP COMMAND-LINE COMMANDS REQUIRES TCP/IP TO BE INSTALLED.

FTP
COMMANDS

BELOW IS A LIST OF COMMAND-LINE FTP (FILE TRANSFER PROTOCOL) COMMANDS FOR *MICROSOFT WINDOWS.*

 TO GET TO THE FTP PROMPT

CLICK ON **START** THEN **RUN** FROM THE START MENU. **TYPE: cmd** IN THE **RUN BOX** AT THE COMMAND PROMPT **TYPE: ftp** AND PRESS ENTER. ftp> WILL COME UP, **TYPE: help** TO GET A LIST OF COMMANDS USED WITH FTP.

FTP (FILE TRANSFER PROTOCOL) USED TO TRANS-
FER FILES TO AND FROM A CLIENT COMPUTER TO AN
FTP SERVER USING THE FILE TRANSFER PROTOCOL

COMMAND LINE PARAMETERS

SYNTAX: ftp [options...]   {host}

SYNTAX:

! [command]

? [command]

- **!** RUNS THE COMMAND YOU SPECIFY.

- **?** DISPLAYS FTP COMMAND HELP DISCRIPTIONS.

- **-a** ALLOWS THE USE OF ANY LOCAL INTERFACE
  WHILE IT BINDS THE DATA CONNECTION.

- **-A** PROVIDES A MEANS OF ANONYMOUS LOGIN.

- **-b** THIS WILL OVERRIDE THE DEFAULT ASYNC
  COUNT VALUE OF 3.

- **-v** REPRESSES THE RESPONSES OF THE REMOTE
  SERVER DISPLAY.

- **-N** REPRESSES UPON THE INITIAL CONNECTION
  THE AUTO LOGIN.

- **-I** DURING MULTIPLE FILE TRANSFERS THIS
  TURNS OFF INTERACTIVE PROMPTING.

- **-d** ALLOWS FOR DEBUGGING AND SHOWS ALL
  OF THE FTP COMMANDS THAT ARE PASSED
  BETWEEN THE CLIENT AND THE SERVER.

- **-g** DISABLES GLOBING BY DEFAULT IT IS ON. GLOBING ALLOWS THE USE OF WILDCARD CHARACTERS IN THE PATH NAMES AND LOCAL FILES.

- **-i** TURNS THE PROMPTING OFF DURING MULTIPLE FILE TRANSFERS. .

- **-n** RESTRAINS THE AUTOMATIC LOGIN WHILE CONNECTING.

- **-v** RESTRAINS VERBOSE DISPLAY OF THE REMOTE SERVER RESPONSES.

- **-s:filename** USE IN THE PLACE OF REDIRECTION. DESIGNATES A FILE THAT CONTAINS FTP COMMANDS. THESE FILES RUN AFTER FTP STARTS.

- **-w:size** Supersede's the default transfer buffer size of 4096.

- **append** APPENDS A LOCAL FILE TO THE REMOTE FILE.

  append [Local-FileName] [RemoteFileName]

- **ascii** SETS THE TRANSFER TYPE AS ASCII, USE ASCII TO TRANSFER TEXT FILES.

  ascii

- **bell** ALLOWS YOU TO ASSIGN A BEEP SOUND WHEN EACH FILE TRANSFER IS COMPLETE.

  bell

- **binary** SETS TRANSFER TYPE TO BINARY (BINARY IMAGE). USE BINARY WHEN TRANSFERING EXECUTABLE FILES.

  binary

- bye   STOPS THE FTP SESSION AND EXITS.   bye

- cd   ALLOWS YOU TO CHANGE THE REMOTE   cd [RemoteDirec-
               WORK ING DIRECTORY   tory]

- close   STOPS FTP SESSION.   close

- debug   Allows you to TOGGLE DEBUGGING   debug
               MODE.

- delete   DELETES A FILE ON THE REMOTE COM   delete [filename]
               PUTER.

- dir   DISPLAYS A LIST OF FILES AND SUBDI   dir [RemoteDi-
               RECTORIES OF THE SREMOTE DIREC   rectory] [local-
               TORY.   filename]

- disconnect   ENDS THE FTP SESSION.   disconnect

- get   GETS A FILE FROM THE REMOTE   get [RemoteFlie]
               COM PUTER THEN SAVES TO LOCAL   [LocalFile]
               MACHINE.

- glob   TOGGLES WILDCARD FILE NAME CHAR   glob
               ACTERS

- hash   TOGGLES PRINTING HASH-SIGN (#)   hash
               FOR EVERY DATA BLOCK THAT IS
               TRANSFERRED.

Command	Description	Syntax
• help	RETREIVES DESCRIPTIONS FOR FTP COMMANDS.	help [command]
• lcd	CHANGES THE LOCAL WORKING DIRECTORY.	lcd [directory]
• mdelete	DELETES FILES ON THE REMOTE COMPTER.	mdelete [files...]
• mdir	DISPLAYS A DIRECTORY AND SUBDIRECTORY LIST OF THE REMOTE COMPUTERS FILES.	mdir [remotefiles]
• mget	DOWNLOADS SPECIFIED FILES FROM REMOTE COMPUTER.	mget [files...]
• mkdir	MAKES A NEW DIRECTORY ON THE REMOTE MACHINE.	mkdir [directory]
• mls	SAVES A LIST OF REMOTE FILES TO A FOLDER ON THE LOCAL MACHINE.	mls [remotefiles] [localfiles]
• open	INDICATES THE PORT AND HOST TO CONNECT TO.	open [host] [port]
• prompt	ALLOWS YOU TO DISABLE OR ENABLE THE INTERACTIVE PROMPTING.	prompt
• put	UPLOADS A FILE TO THE REMOTE MACHINE.	put [localfile] [remotefile]

• pwd	DISPLAYS THE REMOTE MACHINES CUR RENT DIRECTORY.	pwd
• quit	ENDS THE FTP SESSION AND EXITS.	quit
• quote	IDENTIFIES ARGUMENTS AND SENDS THEM TO THE REMOTE FTP SERVER.	quote [argument1] argument2
• recv	INDENTIFIES FILE TO DOWNLOAD FROM REMOTE FTP SERVER AND THEN SAVES IT ON THE LOCAL MACHINE.	recv [remotefile] localfile
• remotehelp	DISPLAYS THE REMOTE MACHINES HELP.	remotehelp [command]
• rename	RENAMES A FILE.	rename [oldname] [newname]
• rmdir	DELETES A DIRECTORY FROM THE REMOTE MACHINE.	rmdir [directory]
• send	UPLOADS A FILE TO THE REMOTE MACHINE.	send [localfile] [remotefile]
• status	DISPLAYS THE FTP STATUS.	status
• trace	LETS YOU TOGGLES BETWEEN TRACING PACKETS OR NOT.	trace

- type

  DEFAULT TRANSFER TYPE IS ASCII.
  CHOOSE ASCII OR BINARY.

  type [ascii or binary]

- user

  FTP REMOTE SERVER LOG IN.

  user [user] [password] [account]

- verbose

  USE VERBOSE MODE TO DISPLAY MORE
  INFORMATION.

  verbose

WNDOWS REPAIR PROCEDURES

LISTED HERE ARE SOME OF THE MOST REQUESTED RE-PAIR PROCEDURES. A FEW OTHER REASON'S A COMPUTER MIGHT NOT START BESIDES THE ONE'S LISTED BELOW ARE: HARDWARE OR SOFTWARE CONFLICTS, INCORRECT HARD DISK BIOS SETTINGS OR MISSING FILES *WINDOWS* NEEDS IN ORDER TO START CORRECTLY. THE FACT IS THERE ARE MANY REASON'S A COMPUTER MAY NOT START CORRECTLY.

Always make a back up of your personal files and system files before editing or changing any thing.

FIRST STEPS TO TAKE IF XP WON'T BOOT UP

1. CREATE A *WINDOWS* STARTUP DISK

INSERT A BLANK DISK INTO FLOPPY DRIVE

- CLICK ON THE START BUTTON (LOWER LEFT CORNER OF THE SCREEN ON THE TASK BAR)
- IN THE **RUN** BOX TYPE: CMD
- AT THE C:\> PROMPT TYPE: format a:/s
  (THIS WILL FORMAT THE DISK AND COPY THE SYSTEM FILES TO A: DRIVE)

This is assuming that your floppy drive is a:\ and your hard drive is C. If not replace your drive letters for the a:\ or c:\ drives.

NEXT COPY THE FOLLOWING FILES TO THE FLOPPY.

- TYPE: C: (IF NOT ALREADY AT THE C:> PROMPT)

- AT THE c:\> PROMPT TYPE: xcopy c:\i386\ ntldr a:\

- AT THE c:\ PROMPT TYPE: xcopy c:\i386\nt detect.com a:\

- AT THE c:\ PROMPT TYPE: xcopy c:\boot.ni a:\

REBOOT THE COMPUTER WITH THE FLOPPY DISK TO BYPASSES THE ACTIVE PARTITION TO ATTEMPT TO START *WINDOWS*.

2. RESTORE THE "LAST KNOWN GOOD CONFIGURATION"

- REBOOT THEN PRESS F8
- WHEN THE *"ADVANCED OPTIONS MENU"* COMES UP SELECT

LAST KNOWN GOOD CONFIGURATION OPTION AND ENTER.

3. SYSTEM RESTORE

Always make a back up of your personal files and system files before editing or changing any thing.

- REBOOT PRESS **F8** AS IT IS LOADING TO DIS PLAY THE **WINDOWS ADVANCED OPTIONS** MENU

- SELECT **SAFE MODE** AND PRESS ENTER.

- SELECT
    - START
    - PROGRAMS
    - ACCESSORIES
    - SYSTEM TOOLS
    - SYSTEM RESTORE.

SELECT **RESTORE COMPUTER TO AN EARLIER TIME.**

(IF THE ABOVE DOES NOT FIX THE PROBLEM YOU CAN USE THE ALTER NATIVE OPTION BELOW)

4. **RECOVERY CONSOLE**

THIS SHOULD BE THE LAST OPTION TO USE IF ALL OTHER OPTIONS FAILED TO RESOLVE THE ISSUE.

- REBOOT WITH THE *WINDOWS* CD.

- FOLLOW THE PROMPTS.

- SELECT "R" TO START THE RECOVERY CON SOLE.

- FOLLOW THE PROMPTS AND SELECT THE AP PROPRIATE OPTIONS.

A lways make a back up of your personal files and system files before editing or changing any thing.

*U SING THIS METHOD REQUIRES THAT YOU SET YOUR BOOT OPTIONS IN BIOS TO **BOOT FROM CD-ROM.***

CAUTION:

THIS WILL DELETE EVERYTHING ON YOUR HARD DRIVE. BACK UP ALL YOUR DATA FIRST.

SYSTEM RESTORE FROM COMMAND PROMPT

Always make a back up of your personal files and system files before editing or changing any thing.

WHAT SYSTEM RESTORE WILL AND WON'T DO

SYSTEM RESTORE ONLY ROLLS BACK SYSTEM FILES, REGISTRY SETTINGS, BATCH FILES, SCRIPTS AND DIFFERENT TYPES OF EXECUTABLE FILES ALONG WITH PROGRAMS INSTALLED ON YOUR COMPUTER TO A STATE IT WAS PREVIOUSLY IN BEFORE THE ERROR OR ISSUE OCCURRED, JUST REPAIRING THE OPERATING SYSTEM.

RESTORE LEAVES PERSONAL FILES INTACT AND UN-CHANGED. IT IS STILL RECOMMENDED TO BACKUP PERSONAL DATA SINCE THESE FILES ARE NOT BACKED UP DURING THE RESTORE PROCESS AND THERE ARE NO GUARANTEES SOMETHING WONT GO WRONG. SOFTWARE PROGRAMS THAT WERE IN-STALLED AFTER THAT RESTORE POINT WILL NEED TO BE REINSTALLED.

DRIVERS WILL BE REVERTED BACK TO THERE ORIGINAL STATE OF THE XP VERSIONS. UPDATE'S

ARE DELETED AND WILL NEED TO BE RE INSTALLED.

SAFE MODE WORKS BY NOT LOADING ALL OF THE OPERATING SYSTEM DRIVERS. THUS ALLOWING YOU TO MAKE NECESSARY CHANGES TO RESTORE THE OPERATING SYSTEM BACK TO A WORKING ORDER.

Always make a back up of your personal files and system files before editing or changing any thing.

INSTRUCTIONS

BOOT UP TO SAFE MODE WITH COMMAND PROMPT.

- TYPE: c:*Windows*\\system32\\restore\\ rstrui.exe AT THE COMMAND PROMPT AND PRESS ENTER.
- FOLLOW DISPLAYED INSTRUCTIONS.

STEPS TO REPAIR THE BOOT SECTOR

USE THIS OPTION IF XP WON'T START YOU MAY HAVE A CORRUPT OR MISSING BOOT SEC-TOR.

POSSIBLE ERROR MESSAGES YOU MAY RECEIVE ARE:

- "INVALID BOOT.INI"

- "*WINDOWS* COULD NOT START"

RECONFIGURING THE BOOT.INI FILE IS RECOMMEND-ED FOR ERRORS STATING THE THE SYSTEM CAN NOT SEE THE

WINDOWS OPERATING SYSTEM INSTALLATION.

WHEN TRYING TO START YOUR COMPUTER.

TO REPAIR A CORRUPTED OR MISSING *BOOT.INI* FILE USE THE *RECOVERY CONSOLE* VERSION OF THE BOOTCFG UTILITY TO FIX IT.

1. REBOOT WITH THE *WINDOWS* CD TO THE *RECOVERY CONSOLE*.

- SELECT "R" FROM THE MENU.
- AT THE COMMAND PROMPT TYPE: ***bootcfg /list*** AND ENTER. *(TO DISPLAY A LIST OF THE ENTRIES OF YOUR CURRENT BOOT FILE)*
- AT THE COMMAND PROMPT TYPE: ***bootcfg / rebuild*** AND ENTER.
- FOLLOW INSTRUCTIONS ON SCREEN.
- PRESS *"Y"* WHEN ASKED TO ADD TO BOOT LIST.
- ENTER YOUR OPERATING SYSTEM NAME

  EX. MICROSOFT *WINDOWS* HOME EDITION FOR THE *LOAD IDENTIFER*.
- TYPE: **/fastdetect** AND PRESS ENTER WHEN IT ASK YOU TO ENTER THE OPERATING SYSTEM LOAD OPTIONS.
- TYPE: **exit** AND PRESS ENTER TO QUIT RECOVERY.

Always make a back up of your personal files and system files before editing or changing any thing.

SIX COMMANDS TO REPAIR WINDOWS

IF YOU ARE RECEIVING ANY OF THESE ERROR MESSAGES MAKE SURE YOU ENTER THESE

COMMANDS IN THE STEPS GIVEN.

ERROR MESSAGES YOU MAY HAVE RECEIVED:

I. WINDOWS COULD NOT START BECAUSE THE FOLLOWING FILE IS MISSING OR CORRUPT: \WINDOWS\SYSTEM32\CONFIG\SYSTEM

II. WINDOWS COULD NOT START BECAUSE THE BELOW FILE IS MISSING OR CORRUPT: \WINNT\SYSTEM32\NTOSKRNL.EXE

III. WINDOWS COULD NOT START BECAUSE THE BELOW FILE IS MISSING OR CORRUPT: \WINNT\SYSTEM32\HAL.DLL

IV. NTLDR IS MISSING

V. INVALID BOOT.INI

INSTRUCTIONS:

- SET BIOS TO BOOT FROM CD/DVD.

Always make a back up of your personal files and system files before editing or changing any thing.

Make sure you set your boot opions in the BIOS to boot from CD/DVD drive.

- REBOOT WITH THE *WINDOWS* CD TO THE RECOVERY CONSOLE.

- DO NOT PRESS F2 OPTION, CONTINUE TILL YOU SEE THE "R" OPTION.

Windows XP Professional Setup

Welcome to Setup.

This portion of the Setup program prepares *Microsoft(R)*

Windows(R) XP to run on your computer.

- To set up *Windows* now, press ENTER.
- To repair a *Windows* installation using

  Recovery Console, press   R.
- To quit Setup without installing *Windows*, press F3.

THE SIX COMMANDS IN THE LEFT HAND COLUMN PUT IN THE SEQUENCE GIVEN WILL ATTEMPT TO FIX THESE ERRORS.

- **Windows** Hardware Abstraction Layer (HAL)

- Corrupt registry hives
 Windows\\SYSTEM32\\CONFIG\\xxxx

- Invalid BOOT.INI files

- A corrupt NTOSKRNL.EXE

- A missing NT Loader (NTLDR)

IMPORTANT

For *Windows make sure you use the /fastdetect as the OS Load Option as the rebuild process is* finalizing.

If you have a *Intel XD or AMD's NX* cpu buffer overflow protection, then you need to also use this.

/noexecute=optin AS THE

OS LOAD OPTION.

DO NOT USE NOEXECUTE FOR THE LOAD OPTION IF YOU DO NOT HAVE THESE CPU'S MENTIONED ABOVE.

- SELECT "R" FROM THE MENU TO START THE *RECOVERY CONSOLE.*

- SELECT INSTALLATION NUMBER (NORMALLY 1 SHOWN ON NEXT PAGE)

- ENTER ADMIN PASSWORD AND ENTER (IF REQUIRED)

- MAKE SURE YOUR IN THE ROOT DIRECTORY (NORMALLY C:\)

- ENTER THE COMMANDS ALL IN A SEQUENCE FROM THE ILLISTRATION IN THE BLACK BOX BELOW.

- FOR THE BOOTCFG /REBUILD AT THE COMMAND PROMPT TYPE: bootcfg /rebuild AND ENTER.

- FOLLOW INSTRUCTIONS ON SCREEN.

- PRESS "Y" WHEN ASKED TO ADD TO BOOT
  LIST.

- ENTER YOUR OPERATING SYSTEM NAME
  EX. MICROSOFT *WINDOWS* HOME EDITION FOR
  THE LOAD IDENTIFER.

- TYPE: /fastdetect AND PRESS ENTER WHEN IT
  ASK YOU TO ENTER THE OPERATING SYSTEM
  LOAD OPTIONS.

- TYPE: exit AND PRESS ENTER TO QUIT RECOV
  ERY.

Always back up system files before editing them.

```
1.  c:\Windows

Which Windows installation would you like to  log onto
(To cancel, press Enter)?  1
Type the Administrator password: ******
c:\Windows>cd..
 c:\>attrib -h -r -s  c : \boot.ini
 c:\>del  boot.ini
 c:\>bootcfg /rebuild

Scanning all disks for Windows installations.

    Please wait, this may take a while...

The Windows installation scan was successful.

Note: The results are stored statically for this seession.
Some message will appear.
Total indentified Windows installs: 1
[1]:  c:\Windows
Add the installation to the boot list? (Yes/No/All):  Y
Enter the Load Identifier:  Microsoft Windows Home Edition
Enter the OS Load Options:

                   /fastdetect  /noexecute=optin
c:\>
c:\>chkdsk  /r  /p
c:\>fixboot

Sure you want to write new bootsector to partition C: ?>  Y
```

- TYPE: exit TO REBOOT.

 - THE CD.. (WITH TWO DOTS) TAKES YOU FROM
 C:*WINDOWS* TO C:\\ .

- THE attrib -h -r -s c:\boot.ini MODIFIES
 THE BOOT.INI FILES SO THEY ARE NOT HIDDEN
 -H, REMOVES THE READ ONLY ATTRIBUTE -R,
 AND REMOVES THE FLAG SETTING IT AS AN
 UNDELETABLE SYSTEM FILE -S.
- THE C:\>del boot.ini DELETES THE BOOT.INI
 FILE AFTER CHANGING ITS ATTRIBUTES.
- THE C:\>bootcfg /rebuild SEARCHES FOR
 THE OPERATING SYSTEM THEN REBUILDS VARI
 OUS CRITICAL COMPONENTS OF THE OPERATING
 SYSTEM.
- THE c:\>chkdsk /r /f CHECKS FOR BAD
 SECTORS AND ANY OTHER ISSUES THAT MAY BE
 CAUSING PROBLEMS.
- THE c:\>fixboot RESTORES THE BOOT SECTOR.

HOW TO RE-INSTALL SYSTEM RESTORE

PERSONAL FILES SUCH AS DOCUMENTS, EMAIL, PHOTOS AND OTHER PERSONAL DATA IS LEFT INTACTED WITH NO CHANGES MADE TO THEM AT ALL.
RESTORE DOES NOT BACK UP PERSONAL FILES AND DATA.

TO REINSTALL THE SYTEM RESTORE FOLLOW THE DIRECTIONS BELOW.

- CLICK THE START BUTTON ON THE DESKTOP, CLICK ON RUN THEN TYPE %windir%\inf.

- RIGHT CLICK ON THE sr.ini FILE AND CHOOSE INSTALL FROM THE MENU.

- AS *WINDOWS* ATTEEMPTS TO INSTALL THE SYSTEM RESTORE IT MAY PROMPT YOU FOR THE PATH TO WHICH IT WILL BE GOING. IF SO THE PATH IS %windir%servicepackfiles.

- AFTER INSTALLATION RESTART *WINDOWS*.WHEN PROMPTED.

Caution:
This will remove all restore points and reset's back to default value.

TO VIEW THE SYSTEM FILE EXTENSIONS, FOLLOW THE INSTRUCTIONS BELOW.

- CLICK THE FOLDER OPTIONS ON THE TOOLS MENU IN THE MY COMPUTER SECTION.
- CLICK THE VIEW TAB.
- UNCHECK THE HIDE EXTENSIONS FOR KNOWN SYSTEM FILE TYPES.

THINGS TO DO BEFORE A WINDOWS REPAIR INSTALL

WARNING:

A POWER FAILURE DURING THE REPAIR INSTALL COULD RENDER YOUR COMPUTER USELESS CAUSING IT NOT TO BOOT UP.

IN PLACE UPGRADE IS ANOTHER OPTION THAT WILL GENERATE THE SAME RESULTS AS THE REPAIR INSTALL.

BEFORE DOING THE REPAIR INSTALL YOU SHOULD DO A BACKUP OF *Windows\ system32\wpa.dbl* _AND_ *Windows\system32\wpa. bak* TO A FLOPPY DISK.

MAKE A BACKUP COPY OF THE REGISTRY FILES LOCATED IN YOUR SYSTEM ROOT REPAIR FOLDER TO A EXTERNAL SOURCE BEFORE USING THE REPAIR INSTALL.

THE INSTRUCTIONS JUST BELOW IS ONLY TO BE USED IF YOU CAN STILL BOOT INTO *WINDOWS*.

1. BEFORE DOING THE REPAIR INSTALL *CLICK ON START THEN RUN.*
- IN THE RUN BOX TYPE: CMD AND ENTER.
- AT THE COMMAND PROMPT TYPE: del /a /f c:\ *Windows*\system32\undo_guimode.txt

IF YOU RECEIVE AN ERROR MESSAGE STATING THAT THE SETUP CAN NOT CONTINUE BECAUSE OF AN EARLIER VERSION IS TRYING TO BE INSTALLED THEN FOLLOW THE INSTRUCTIONS BELOW:

- GO INTO THE ADD/REMOVE SECTION OF THE CONTROL PANEL AND REMOVE THE SP1 AND/OR SP2 UPDATES FIRST.

HOW TO DO A
WINDOWS
REPAIR INSTALL

THE REPAIR INSTALL WILL USE THE FILES ON THE *WINDOWS* CD TO REPLACE THE SYSTEM FILES THAT WERE ALTERED ON YOUR COMPUTER, INCLUDING FILES ALTERED BY MALWARE AND ADWARE.

YOU WILL NEED TO REINSTALL ANY UPDATES AS THESE WILL NOT BE LEFT ON YOUR COMPUTER AFTER THIS REPAIR. YOUR PERSONAL FILES AND SETTINGS WILL BE UNAFFECTED. ALTHOUGH IT IS STRONGLY RECOMMEND-ED TO DO A BACKUP OF ALL YOUR PERSONAL DATA THAT YOU WANT SAVED TO AN EXTERNAL SOURCE.

THE "IN PLACE UP-GRADE" IS ANOTHER OPTION THAT WILL GENERATE THE SAME AS THE REPAIR INSTALL.

1. REBOOT WITH THE *WINDOWS* CD AND PRESS ENTER TO START *WINDOWS SETUP*. DO NOT CHOOSE REPAIR USING *RECOVERY CONSOLE* WITH THE "R" OPTION.

• ACCEPT THE LICENSE AGREEMENT TO START THE SEARCH FOR THE *WINDOWS* INSTALLATIONS.

• SELECT THE CORRECT *WINDOWS* INSTALLATION THEN PRESS "R" THIS WILL START THE REPAIR PRO-CESS.

RECONFIGUR-ING THE BOOT.INI FILE IS RECOMMENDED FOR ERRORS STATING THE THE SYSTEM CAN NOT SEE THE *WIN-DOWS* OPERATING SYSTEM INSTALLA-TION.

• END THE SETUP PROCESS IF THE OPTION FOR RE-PAIR IS NOT A CHOICE. YOU WILL NOT BE ABLE TO USE THIS AS A REPAIR OPTION. YOU COULD RENDER YOUR COMPUTER USELESS, DELETING ALL DATA AND HAVING TO REINSTALL *WINDOWS*.

- ALL FILES NECESSARY WILL BE COPIED TO THE HARD DRIVE THEN REBOOT ON ITS OWN.

- WHEN MESSAGE APPEARS TO BOOT FROM CD DO NOT BOOT FROM CD. SETUP WILL CONTINUE.

- IF ANY ERROR MESSAGES ARE DISPLAYED ABOUT FILES NOT FOUND, ACTIVATE THE *WINDOWS FIREWALL* FIRST BEFORE CONNECTING TO THE INTERNET.

- TO ACTIVATE THE FIREWALL
    - *CONTROL PANEL*
    - *NETWORK CONNECTIONS*
    - *HIGHLIGHT THE CORRECT CONNECTION THEN RIGHT CLICK.*
    - *SELECT PROPERTIES FROM THE MENU.*
    - *CLICK ON THE ADVANCED TAB AND CHECK THE BOX TO ENABLE THE FIREWALL.*

- NOW CONTINUE WITH THE SETUP TO ACTIVATE OVER THE INTERNET.

- REAPPLY THE SERVICE PACKS (IF NECESSARY) AND THE *WINDOWS* UPDATES.

- REBOOT YOUR COMPUTER.

- CHECK TO SEE IF YOUR RESTORE IS WORKING CORRECTLY. TRY CREATING A RESTORE POINT.

- IF THIS DOES NOT FIX THE ISSUE THEN TRY RECONFIGURING THE BOOT.INI FILE.

- SET BOOT OPTIONS TO BOOT FROM CD/DVD.

- BOOTUP WITH THE *WINDOWS CD.*

- PRESS THE "R" TO LOAD THE *RECOVERY CON SOLE.*

- AT THE PROMPT TYPE: copy x:\i386\ntldr c:\

- AT THE PROMPT TYPE: copy x:\i386\netdetect. com c:\

- AT THE PROMPT TYPE: attrib -h -r -s c:\boot.ini del c:\ boot.ini.

- AT THE PROMPT TYPE: bootcfg /rebuild.

- TYPE: boot.cfg at the command prompt.

  TRY THE *REPAIR INSTALL* AGAIN.

Caution:
ALWAYS BACK UP YOUR PERSONAL FILES BEFORE MAKING ANY CHANGES TO YOUR COMPUTER.

ERROR MESSAGES

LISTED BELOW IS A LIST OF ERROR MESSAGES YOU CAN USE WHEN YOU ARE DIAG-NOSING COMPUTER ISSUES.

ERROR MESSAGE	SUGGESTIONS
BAD SECTOR READ/WRITE ERROR MESSAGE	• USE SCANDISK TO TRY TO REPAIR THE DISK. • FORMAT THE DISK IF REPAIRS CAN NOT BE MADE WITH SCANDISK.

WARNING FORMATTING YOUR COMPUTER WILL ERASE EVERTHING ON IT. MAKE A BACK-UP COPY FIRST BEFORE ATTEMPTING THIS.

IF YOU ARE EXPERI-ENCING A PROBLEM WITH *WINDOWS* WHILE IT IS LOADING OR PREVENT-ING IT FROM LOADING THEN YOU ARE PROABLEY DEALING WITH A CON-FIGURATION ERROR IN THE REGISTRY.

ERROR MESSAGES DURING BOOT BEFORE LOADING *WINDOWS*

• MAKE SURE THAT YOUR BIOS SET-TINGS ARE CONFIGURED CORRECTLY FOR THE HARDWARE THAT IS ON YOUR COMPUTER.

ERROR MESSAGES THAT OCCUR BEFORE OR AFTER THE OPERATING SYSTEM IS LOADING CAN BE CAUSED BY A VIRUS, A CONFLICT WITH AN-OTHER PROGRAM TRYING TO LOAD AT THE SAME TIME, OR YOU NOT CON-FIGURING A HARDWARE DEVICE CORRECTLY.

Error Message	Suggestions
BAD COMMAND	• CHECK THE PATH TO MAKE SURE IT IS CORRECT. • CHECK THE SPELLING. • MAKE SURE YOUR VERSION OF DOS IS THE CORRECT ONE FOR THE COMMAND BEING USED.
BAD OR MISSING COMMAND INTERPRETER	• A PRIOR VERSION OF COMMAND. COM EXISTS. • COMMAND.COM HAS BEEN DELETED. • OPERATING SYSTEM CAN NOT LOCATE COMMAND.COM • TYPE: fdisk /mbr TO REPAIR THE MASTER BOOT RECORD.

DOS

DISK OPERATING SYSTEM.

THE NAME OF A OPERATING

SYSTEM PRODUCED BY DIFFERENT MANUFACTURES. MS-DOS WAS PRODUCED BY *MICROSOFT* FOR THE 16BIT MICROCOMPUTERS.

ERROR MESSAGE	SUGGESTIONS
BAD COMMAND	• CHECK THE PATH TO MAKE SURE IT IS CORRECT. • CHECK THE SPELLING. • MAKE SURE YOUR VERSION OF DOS IS THE CORRECT ONE FOR THE COMMAND BEING USED.
BAD OR MISSING COMMAND INTERPRETER	• A PRIOR VERSION OF COMMAND.COM EXISTS. • COMMAND.COM HAS BEEN DELETED. • OPERATING SYSTEM CAN NOT LOCATE COMMAND.COM • TYPE: fdisk /mbr TO REPAIR THE MASTER BOOT RECORD.
BAD OR MISSING FILE	• CHECK THAT THE FILE EXIST. • CHECK THAT THE PATH IS CORRECT. • CHECK THAT THE CORRECT FILE VERSION IS BEING USED. • MAKE SURE THE SPELLING IS CORRECT.
BAD OR MISSING OPERATING SYSTEM	• GO TO CHAPTER *WINDOWS* REPAIR COMMANDS MISSING OR CORRUPT BOOT SECTOR.

ERROR MESSAGE	SUGGESTIONS
BAD OR MISSING OPERATING SYSTEM	• GO TO CHAPTER *WINDOWS* REPAIR COMMANDS MISSING OR CORRUPT BOOT SECTOR.
BEEPS DURING START-UP	• TURN TO THE CHAPTER ABOUT BEEP CODES. • GO TO THE MANUFACTURE OF THE MOTHERBOARD'S WEB SITE.
BLUE SCREEN	• PRESS SPACEBAR TO BOOT TO THE "LAST KNOWN GOOD CONFIGURA-TION". • REBOOT AND PRESS F8 TO GET TO LAST KNOWN GOOD CONFIGURATION.
CAN NOT FIND BOOT-ABLE CD-ROM DEVICE	• CHANGE BIOS BOOT SEQUENCE.
CAN NOT FIND SYSTEM FILES	• MAKE SURE YOUR IN THE RIGHT DIRECTORY WHERE THE FILES ARE LOCATED.
CHECKSUM ERROR	• CHANGE THE CMOS BATTERY.
CMOS CONFIGURATION ERROR	• CHECK CMOS FOR ERRORS. • MAKE SURE THE HARDWARE INSTALLED MATCHES THAT OF CMOS.
CMOS CONFIGURATION MISMATCH	• WRITE DOWN EVERYTHING IN CMOS THEN ERASE AND RECONFIGURE WITH THE CORRECT INFORMATION.

SECTOR

EACH DISK HAS TRACKS ON IT. EACH TRACK HAVING SECTORS.

ERROR MESSAGE	SUGGESTIONS
CORRUPT OR MISSING FILES	• TYPE: **sfc /scannow** TO SCAN *WINDOWS* SYSTEM FILES FOR MISSING OR CORRUPT OPERATING SYSTEM FILES THEN REPLACES THEM WITH THE CORRECT *MICROSOFT* VERSIONS.
DEVICE DRIVER NOT FOUND	• MAKE SURE THE CD-ROM IS CONNECTED. • MAKE SURE THE CD-ROM DRIVER SHOWS UP IN CONFIG.SYS.
DIRECTORY ALREADY EXIST	• CHANGE THE NAME TO SOME-THING ELSE. DIRECTORY ALREADY HAS A NAME WITH THE ONE YOUR ARE TRYING TO USE.
DISK BOOT FAILURE	• BOOT FROM A FLOPPY AND TYPE: **sys c:** TO ADD SYSTEM FILES TO THE FLOPPY.
DISK FULL	• THE DISK IS FULL, TRY A NEW ONE OR REMOVE FILES FROM THE DISK.
DRIVE A: NOT READY, ABORT, RETRY, FAIL	• DRIVE IS DIRTY • FLOPPY DRIVE IS BAD • DISK IS CORRUPT • DISK IS LOCKED

ERROR MESSAGE	SUGGESTIONS
DRIVE DOES NOT EXIST	• FLOPPY DISK DRIVE MAY BE DIRTY. • FLOPPY DRIVE MAY BE BAD. • FLOPPY DISK CONTROLLER MAY BE BAD.
DUPLICATE FILE NAME OR FILE NOT FOUND	• CHECK SPELLING • CHECK TO SEE IF THE FILE YOUR TRYING TO NAME IS ALREADY IN THE DIRECTORY.
ERROR 600 MESSAGE	THIS IS AN INTERNAL ERROR. • CHECK TO SEE IF ALL YOUR DEVICES ARE FUNCTIONAL. • MAKE SURE THE NETWORK CONFIGURATION IS CORRECT. • COULD MEAN AN OPERATION IS PENDING.
ERROR 601 MESSAGE	THIS IS AN IITERNAL ERROR. • SYSTEM HAS DETECTED AN INVALID PORT. • CHECK TO SEE IF ALL YOUR DEVICES ARE FUNCTIONAL. • MAKE SURE THE NETWORK CONFIGURATION IS CORRECT.

ERROR MESSAGE	SUGGESTIONS
ERROR 602 MESSAGE	THIS MEANS THAT A PORT IS ALREADY OPEN. • FAX OR OTHER PROGRAM IS USING THE PORT. • CLOSE THE PROGRAM USING THE PORT.
ERROR 603 MESSAGE	THIS IS AN INTERNAL ERROR DEALING WITH CALLER'S BUFFER IS TO SMALL. • CHECK TO SEE IF ALL YOUR DEVICES ARE FUNCTIONAL. • MAKE SURE THE NETWORK CONFIGURATION IS CORRECT.
ERROR 611 MESSAGE	THIS ERROR IS CAUSED BY THE NETWORK CONFIGURATION NOT BEING CORRECT POSSIBABLY THE ROUTE SPECIFIED WAS NOT AVAILABLE. • REBOOT AND CHECK TO SEE IF ALL THE RECENTLY APPLIED CONFIG-RATIONS HAVE BEEN APPLIED.
ERROR 627 MESSAGE	THIS ERROR INDICATES THAT A KEY WAS NOT LOCATED. • CHECK TO SEE IF THE CORRECT NETWORK CONFIGURATIONS ARE SET. • MAKE SURE THAT THE MODEM YOUR USING IS SUPPORTED.

ERROR MESSAGE	SUGGESTIONS
ERROR 628 MESSAGE	THIS ERROR MESSAGE INDICATES THAT THE CONNECTION WAS CLOSED. • CONNECTION CLOSED BY REMOTE COMPUTER. • FOR DIAL-UP MAKE SURE THE PHONE NUMBER IS CORRECT. • IF TRYING TO CONNECT TO A VPN THEN MAKE SURE THAT THE SECURITY SETTINGS ARE CORRECT.
ERROR 629 MESSAGE	THIS ERROR INDICATES THAT THE REMOTE COMPUTER HAS CLOSED THE CONNECTION. CAUSES FOLLOW. • LINE NOISE. • ERROR WITH THE PHONE LINE. • CONNECTION SPEED CONFIGURED WRONG. • SYSTEM ADMINISTRATOR HAS DISCONNECTED THE CONNECTION.

ERROR MESSAGE	SUGGESTIONS
ERROR 630 MESSAGE	THIS ERROR INDICATES HARDWARE FAILURE CAUSING THE MODEM TO BE DISCONNECTED. • CHECK TO SEE IF YOUR MODEM CABLE IS PLUGGED IN. • CHECK TO SEE IF THE MODEM IS TURNED ON. • AN ERROR HAS OCCURRED IN THE MODEM OR OTHER COMMUNICATION DEVICE. • MODEM NEEDS REPLACED.

ERROR MESSAGE	SUGGESTIONS
ERROR 636 MESSAGE	THIS ERROR IS CAUSED BY A DEVICE THAT IS ATTACHED TO THE PORT IS NOT THE ONE EXPECTED. • CHECK TO SEE IF THE HARDWARE SETTINGS ARE THE CORRECT CONFIGURATION SETTINGS THAT YOUR COMPUTER HAS SET FOR IT. **INSTRUCTIONS ON HOW TO CHANGE SETTINGS FOR A CONNECTION.** – CLICK START THEN *CONTROL PANEL* THEN *NETWORK AND INTERNET CONNECTIONS* THEN *NETWORK CONNECTIONS*. – SELECT THE CONNECTION YOU WANT TO CONFIGURE. – SELECT *NETWORK TASKS* THEN CLICK ON "CHANGE SETTINGS OF THIS CONNECTION".
ERROR 639 MESSAGE	• *NETBIOS* SETTINGS ARE INCORRECT. • REBOOT AND CHECK TO SEE IF HARDWARE SETTINGS ARE CONSISTIANT WITH COMPUTERS SETTINGS.

ERROR MESSAGE	SUGGESTIONS
ERROR 641 MESSAGE	THIS ERROR INDICATES AN INCREASE IN RESOURCE CAPACITY WITH THE REMOTE SERVER IS IN NEED. • STOP USE OF UNUSED RESOURCES IN THE *COMPUTER MANAGMENNT* PART OF THE *SERVICES* SELECTION. • INCREASE RESOURCES OF *REMOTE ACCESS SERVER.*
ERROR 642 MESSAGE	THIS ERROR INDICATES THAT ANOTHER MACHINE WITH THE SAME NAME IS ALREADY LOGGED ON THE REMOTE SERVER NETWORK. • MAKE SURE YOUR NOT ALREADY CONNECTED TO THE NETWORK YOU ARE TRYING TO CONNECT TO. • CHECK TO SEE IF A MACHINE WITH THE SAME NAME IS LISTED ON THE NETWORK.
ERROR 643 MESSAGE	• INDICATION OF A FAILED NET-WORK ADAPTER AT THE SERVER.

ERROR MESSAGE	SUGGESTIONS
ERROR 678 MESSAGE	• MODEM IS NOT RECEIVING A DIAL TONE. • COULD BE DIALLING THE WRONG NUMBER. • MODEM ON THE RECEIVING END MAY NOT BE ANSWERING. TO CHECK DIAL THE NUMBER TO SEE IF YOU RECEIVE A MODEM TONE. IF SO THIS IS NOT THE PROBLEM.

ERROR MESSAGE	SUGGESTIONS
ERROR 711 MESSAGE	• *TELEPHONY SERVICES* MAY NOT BE STARTED. • *PLUG AND PLAY (PNP)* MAY NOT BE STARTED. • *REMOTE ACCESS AUTO CONNECTION MANAGER* MAY NEED TO BE STARTED. • *REMOTE ACCESS CONNECTION MANAGER* MAY NEED TO BE STARTED. **TO START ANY ONE OF THESE SERVICES OPEN THE *ADMINISTRATIVE TOOLS*.** • *DOUBLE CLICK ON THE SERVICES.* • RIGHT CLICK ON A SERVICE THAT IS LISTED ABOVE AND CLICK ON PROPERTIES. • ON THE *GENERAL TAB* SELECT MANUAL NEXT TO *STARTUP TYPE.* • CLICK ON THE APPLY BUTTON THEN CLICK THE *START.*

ERROR MESSAGE	SUGGESTIONS
ERROR 733 MESSAGE	**THIS ERROR MESSAGE IS NORMALLY ASSOCIATED WITH THE DIAL-UP CONNECTION.** • DISABLE THE *NEGOTATE MULTI-ILINK* FOR *SINGLE LINK CONNECTIONS.* • OPEN *NETWORK CONNECTIONS.* • RIGHT CLICK DIAL-UP CONNECTIONS. • RIGHT CLICK ON PROPERTIES. • CLICK ON THE OPTIONS TAB. • CLICK THE *PPP* SETTINGS. • CLEAR THE CHECK BOX FOR *NEGO- TIATE MULTI LINK FOR SINGLE LINK CONNECTIONS.* AND CLICK OK. • CLICK OK IN THE NETWORK CONNECTIONS THEN EXIT.
FATAL WRITE ERROR	• CONNECT TO THE NETWORK DRIVE.
FILE CAN NOT BE COPIED ONTO ITSELF	• YOU MAY OF FORGOTTEN TO SPECIFY THE DESTINATION DIRECTORY THE FILE IS SUPPOSE TO BE COPIED TO.

ERROR MESSAGE	SUGGESTIONS
FILE CREATION ERROR	• DISK MAY BE WRITE PROTECTED. UNLOCK DISK ON BACK. • YOUR TRYING TO NAME A FILE WITH A NAME THAT ALREADY EXIST.
FILE NOT FOUND	• MAKE SURE THE SPELLING IS CORRECT. • CHECK TO SEE IF THE FILE EXIST. • MAKE SURE THE PATH IS COR-RECT.
FIXED DISK ERROR	• OPERATING SYSTEM CAN NOT FIND THE HARD DISK. • CONTROLLER CARD NOT RESPONDING.
FORMATTING WHILE COPING	• TRY FORMATTING THE DISK BEFORE COPING FILES TO IT. IT TAKES A LOT LONGER TO FORMAT WHILE COPING.
HARD MEMORY ERROR	• CAUSED BY PERMANENT PHYSICAL FAILURES WHICH GENERATE NMI ERRORS. REQUIRES MEMORY UNIT TO BE CHECKED BY SUBSTITUTION.

ERROR MESSAGE	SUGGESTIONS
HARD DRIVE NOT FOUND	• CHECK SETUP INFORMATION IN BIOS TO SEE IF IT IS CORRECT. • MAKE SURE THE RIGHT HARD DRIVE IS LISTED IN BIOS. • MAKE SURE THE CONNECTIONS ARE SEATED PROPERLY. • MAKE SURE CABLES HAVE NOT COME LOOSE. • SWAP THE POWER SUPPLY WITH A KNOWN GOOD ONE.
HELP NOT AVAILABLE FOR THIS COMMAND	• THE COMMAND DOES NOT HAVE A HELP FILE ASSOCIATED WITH IT. • COULD OF TYPED IN THE COMAND WRONG.
INCORRECT DOS VERSION	• MAKE SURE THE COMMAND FOR THE PROGRAM YOU ARE TRYING TO RUN MATCHES THE VERSION OF DOS INSTALLED ON YOUR COMPUTER. • INSTALL SOFTWARE PROGRAMS THAT HAVE THE SAME DOS VERSION THAT YOU ARE RUNNING.

Error Message	Suggestions
Insufficient memory	• Close applications that are not in use. • Reboot.
Insufficient disk space	• Not enough space on hard drive, try deleting files not needed. • Install an additional hard drive.
Invalid boot.ini	• Configure bios to boot from CD-ROM • Boot from *Windows* CD • Start the recovery console
Invalid date or time	• The format for time and date is wrong. Reset with proper settings.
Invalid directory	• Make sure the name you typed is spelled correctly. • Directory does not exist. Create a new directory with the name your trying to go to.

Error Message	Suggestions
Invalid drive error	• Check to see if CMOS is listing your disk. • Hard drive may have a corrupt partition table.
Invalid drive in search path	• Update the path command in AUTOEXEC.BAT.
Invalid drive specification	• Drive doesn't exist. • You typed in the wrong drive letter. • Drive specified is not working. • If error message is when switching to another hard drive, hard drive may have a corrupt partition.
Invalid file name	• File doesn't exist. • Spelling is wrong for the file specified.
Invalid media type	• Floppy is not formatted right for your floppy drive. • Floppy disk not formatted.
Invalid or missing COMMAND.COM	• Remove non booting disk from drive and reboot. • Copy COMMAND.COM from a floppy disk to the C:\ drive.
IO.SYS is missing or bad	• Insert startup disk and reboot.

ERROR MESSAGE	SUGGESTIONS
MISSING OPERATING SYSTEM	• NON-BOOTABLE DISK IN FLOPPY DRIVE.
MISSING OPERATING SYSTEM, ERROR LOADING OPERATING SYSTEM	• MBR CAN NOT READ THE BOOT SECTOR ON ACTIVE PARTITION. • BOOT FROM A START-UP DISK.
NO BOOT DEVICE AVAILABLE	• BOOT WITH A START-UP DISK. • HARD DISK MAY NEED TO BE FORMATTED.
NO OPERATING SYSTEM	• RUN SYS.COM FROM THE BOOT DISK. • RUN REPAIR.COM. • RUN FORMAT /MBR OR FORMAT C: /C:
NON-ASKABLE INTERRUPT ERROR	• DEFECTIVE RAM.

ERROR MESSAGE	SUGGESTIONS
NON-SYSTEM DISK OR DISK ERROR	<ul><li>NON-SYSTEM DISK IS IN FLOPPY DRIVE, REMOVE AND REBOOT.</li><li>COMMAND.COM OR SYSTEM HIDDEN FILES ARE CORRUPT OR MISSING .</li><li>BOOT WITH A DOS START-UP DISK AND COPY THE SYSTEM FILES TO THE C:\ DRIVE<ul><li>AT THE A:\ TYPE: C: AND PRESS ENTER. IF THE C:\ PROMPT COMES UP THEN THE DRIVE IS THERE BUT THE OPERATING SYSTEM IS LOST.</li><li>AT THE C:\> DOS PROMPT TYPE: cd dos AND PRESS ENTER.</li><li>AT THE PROMPT TYPE: SYS C: AND PRESS ENTER. THIS SHOULD REPLACE THE OPERATING SYSTEM.</li><li>IF INVALID DRIVE SPECIFICATION MESSAGE COMES UP WHEN CHANGING TO THE C:\ DRIVE THEN THE HARD DRIVE IS DEFECTIVE.</li></ul></li></ul>
NOT READY READING DRIVE A: ABORT, RETRY, FAIL?	<ul><li>NO DISK IN DRIVE A:</li><li>DISK IN DRIVE A IS CORRUPT, MISSING OR NEEDS FORMATTED.</li><li>INSERT NEW DISK.</li></ul>

Error Message	Suggestions
NTDETECT .COM	• Boot file is missing or corrupt. • Go to the chapter *Windows* repair command for missing or corrupt boot.ini file.
Out of memory error	• System needs more free memory. • Dynamic swap file is limited due to the small amount of free space on your host drive.

Page fault	• Occurs when memory manager doesn't provide
	    the memory requested thereby is forced to use virtual
	    memory.
	
	• Try increasing the virtual memory on your computer.

Parity error	• Faulty ram.
Path not found	• Path does not exist. • Path typed incorrectly.
Press F1 to continue	• Need to correct the configuration information.

ERROR MESSAGE	SUGGESTIONS
WINDOWS COULD NOT START BECAUSE THE FOLLOWING FILE IS MISSING OR CORRUPT: WINDOWS\SYSTEM32\HAL.DLL	THE BOOT.INI FILE COULD BE MISSING, CONTAINS INCORRECT INFORMATION OR IS DAMAGED. TO FIX:

THE BOOT.INI FILE COULD BE MISSING, CONTAINS INCORRECT INFORMATION OR IS DAMAGED. TO FIX:

1. SET BIOS TO BOOT FROM CD/DVD.

2. REBOOT WITH THE WINDOWS CD.

3. START THE RECOVERY CONSOLE.

4. PRESS THE "R" AT THE WELCOME TO SETUP MESSAGE.

5. FOLLOW INSTRUCTIONS.

6. AT THE PROMPT TYPE: bootcfg /list AND THEN ENTER.

7. AT THE PROMPT TYPE: bootcfg /rebuild THEN ENTER AFTER IT SCANS FOR THE OPERATING SYSTEM IT WILL DISPLAY THE RESULTS.

8. TO ADD THE WINDOWS INSTALLATION TO THE BOOT.INI FILE JUST FOLLOW THE ON SCREEN INSTRUCTIONS.

9. ENTER MICROSOFT WINDOWS PROFESSIONAL OR MICROSOFT WINDOWS HOME EDITION WHEN YOU SEE THE "ENTER LOAD IDENTIFIER" AND PRESS ENTER.

10. TYPE: /fastdetect AND PRESS ENTER WHEN YOU SEE THE MESSAGE "ENTER OS LOAD OPTIONS".

11. TYPE: EXIT AND PRESS ENTER.

ERROR MESSAGE	SUGGESTIONS
WRITE-PROTECT ERROR WRITING DRIVE A:	• FLOPPY DISK IS WRITE PROTECTED. UNLOCK ON BACK OF FLOPPY UPPER LEFT CORNER.

**IRQ
TABLE**

IRQ (INTERRUPT REQUEST) ALLOWS IN-PUT AND OUTPUT DEVICES TO INTRUPT THE
CPU.

▩ IRQs AND SERIAL PORTS

• IRQs AND INPUT AND OUTPUT PORT ADDRESSES CAN BE SET TO ANY ONE OF THE FOUR SERIAL PORT COMBINATIONS OR PARALLEL CONNECTIONS.

IRQ	I/O ADDRESS (IN HEX)	PORT	TYPE
• IRQ4	03F8-3FF	COM1	SERIAL
• IRQ3	02F8-2FF	COM2	SERIAL
• IRQ4	03E8-3EF	COM3	SERIAL
• IRQ3	02E8-2EF	COM4	SERIAL
• IRQ7	0378-37F	LPT1	PARALLEL
• IRQ5	0278-27F	LPT2	PARALLEL

IRQ	I/O ADDRESS	COMMON USE	RESOURCE TYPE	MOST RECOMMENED USES
0	040-05F	SYSTEM TIMER	SYSTEM	RESERVED FOR SYSTEM ONLY
1	060-06F	KEYBOARD CONTROLLER	SYSTEM	RESERVED FOR SYSTEM ONLY
2	0A0-0-AF	SECOND IRQ CONTROLLER CASCADES IRQ 8-15	SYSTEM	RESSERVED FOR SYSTEM ONLY
3	— —	COM2 SERIAL PORT 2	— —	MODEM
4	— —	COM1 SERIAL PORT 1	— —	COM1
5	— —	LPT2 PARALLEL PORT 2	— —	SOUND CARD
6	— —	FLOPPY DISK CONTROLLER	SYSTEM	FLOPPY DISK CONTROLLER

LPT1, LPT2, LPT3

LPT1 IS A FILE NAME *WINDOWS* AND DOS REFERS TO AS THE FIRST PARALLEL PRINTR PORT. OTHER PARALLEL PORTS ARE KNOWN AS LPT2 & LPT3.

mode lpt1:=com1:

SETS THE LPT1 EQUAL TO THE FIRST SERIAL PORT COM1.

IRQ	I/O ADDRESS	COMMON USE	RESOURCE TYPE	MOST RECOMMENED USES
7	— —	LPT1 Parallel port 1	— —	LPT1
8	070-07F	Real time clock	System	Reserved for system Only
9	— —	Mostly used for Peripherals often shows up as IRQ2	PCI	Network interface card, PCI device, VGA,
10	— —	Mostly used for Peripherals	PCI	USB
11	— —	Available	PCI	SCSI host adapter, PCI device
12	238-23F	Available - Mouse port	ISA/PCI	Mouse port or motherboard

SCSI (Small computer system interface) Up to 7 device's that require high speed transfer like harddisk, scanner or CD-ROM drive can be linked to a single SCSI port.

IRQ	I/O ADDRESS	COMMON USE	RESOURCE TYPE	MOST RECOMMENED USES
13	0F8-0-FF	MATH COPROCESSOR	SYSTEM	RESERVED FOR THE SYSTEM ONLY
14	1F0-1F7	PRIMARY IDE CHANNEL - AVAILABLE	PCI	HARD DISK, SCSI HOST ADAPTER
15	170-170	SECONDARY IDE CHANNEL - AVAILABLE	PCI	CD/DVD-ROM OR TAPE DRIVE

BEEP CODES

BELOW IS A LIST OF BEEP CODES AND OR BIOS ERROR MESSAGES. WHEN COMPUTER FAILS TO POWER ON AFTER RECEIVING A BEEP CODE AT BOOT UP MEANS YOUR SYSTEM IS REPORTING A IMPORTANT HARDWARE ERROR.

NOT ALL MANUFACTURES USE BEEP CODES. *AWARD* BIOS USES BEEP CODES ONLY FOR VIDEO ISSUES. CODE CAN BE READ WITH A POST DIAGNOSTICS CARD OR ERROR MESSAGES BEING DISPLAYED ON THE SCREEN.

THESE ARE THE BEEP CODES FOR SOME OF THE MAIN BIOS MANUFACTURERS. IF YOUR'S IS NOT LISTED HERE THEN CONTACT THE MANUFACTURES WEB SITE FOR MORE INFORMATION. A LIST OF MANUFACTURES WILL FOLLOW THE CODES. TO DETERMINE WHAT MANUFACTURE YOU HAVE JUST RE-BOOT THE COMPUTER, MOST COMPUTER'S WILL SHOW THE NAME OF THE BIOS MANUFACTURES

AMI BIOS BEEP CODES

Beeps	Description	What to Do
1	Memory Refresh Failure.	Check to see if the memory module needs reseat or replaced.
2	Parity error	• Error in base memory in the first 64 KiB block. • Reseat memory mode or replace.
3	Base 64 Memory Error	Read/write test error. * Reseat memory mode or replace.
4	Motherboard	Timer not operational * Check to see if all the PSU to MB connectors are seated. * Motherboard may need to be sent in for repairs.
5	Processor Failure	• Make sure the processor is seated • CPU or Motherboard may need to be replaced or repaired.

BIOS

Basic **I**nput **O**utput **S**ystem

Contains sets of procedures stored on a ROM chip.

The procedures handle hardware input/output functions like the screen graphics.

ROM

Read **O**nly **M**emory

Computer memory that contains instructions that can not be changed.

Beeps	Description	What to Do
6	8042 Gate A20 failure.	Can't switch to protective mode. * Replace keyboard * Reseat keyboard controller chip. * Replace keyboard controller chip.
7	Processor general exception interrupt error	System board may need to be sent in for repairs
8	Video display memory read/write error	• Memory on the video card may need replaced. • Video card may need replaced.
9	ROM checksum error	BIOS chip may need replaced.
10	Register read/write error CMOS shutdown	Motherboard may need to be repaired.

Beeps	Description	What to Do
11	Cache memory bad	• Reset memory card • Replace cache memory

AWARD BIOS POST ERROR MESSAGES

ERROR MESSAGE	DESCRIPTION	WHAT TO DO
1 long 2 SHORT	VIDEO DISPLAY PROBLEMS	• Reset video card. • Replace video card.
BIOS ROM checksum error	CORRUPTED BIOS CODE	• REPLACE BIOS CHIP.
CMOS BATTERY FAILED	THE BATTERY IN CMOS IS BAD.	• REPLACE BATTERY.
CMOS CHECKSUM ERROR	BATTERY COULD BE WEAK OR CMOS MAY HAVE BECOME CORRUPTED.	• REPLACE BATTERY.
FLOPPY DISK FAILED	FLOPPY DISK CAN NOT BE FOUND OR INITIALIZED BY BIOS.	• TRY SWAPPING A KNOWN GOOD FLOPPY DRIVE FOR THE ONE IN QUESTION.
HARD DISK INSTALL FAILED	BIOS CAN NOT FIND THE HARD DISK DRIVE CONTROLLER.	• SWAP A KNOWN GOOD HARD DRIVE FOR THE ONE IN QUESTION.

CMOS RAM

MEMORY THAT STORES CON-FIGURATOIN INFORMATION ABOUT THE COMPUTER.

OPERATED BY A BATTERY THAT KEEPS CERTAIN CON-FIGUREATION INFORMATION FROM BEING ERASED WHEN THE COMPUTER IS TURNED OFF.

ERROR MESSAGE	DESCRIPTION	WHAT TO DO
HARD DISK DIAGNOSTICS HAS FAILED	HARD DRIVE DID NOT PASS THE DOGNOSTICS TEST.	• TROUBLESHOOT THE SUBSYSTEM FOR THE HARD DRIVE
KEYBOARD ERROR OR NO KEYBOARD PRESENT	KEYBOARD CAN NOT BE LOCATED BY BIOS.	• CHECK TO SEE IF THE KEYBOARD IS CONNECTED. • MAKE SURE THE KEYS ARE NOT BEING PRESSED IN. • REPLACE KEY-BOARD.
MEMORY TEST FAILED	MEMORY IS NOT BEING DETECTED.	• RESET THE MEMORY CARD. • REPLACE MEMORY CARD.

DELL BIOS BEEP CODES & ERROR MESSAGES

Beep Code Or Error Message	Description	What to do
1-2	Video card not found	• Try resetting the video card. • Try using the PCI slot. • Install a new video card.
1-2-2-3	ROM BIOS has failed	• Install a new ROM BIOS chip.
1-3-1-1 1-3-3-1 1-3-4-1 1-4-1-1	Memory has failed.	• Check to see if the memory cards are seated properly. • Install new memory cards.

During post before the video is checked ROM BIOS communicates error messages with a series of beeps.

BEEP CODE OR ERROR MESSAGE	DESCRIPTION	WHAT TO DO
1-3-1-3	KEYBOARD CONTROLLER HAS FAILED.	• CHECK TO SEE IF THE KEYBOARD CONNECTOR ON THE MOTHER-BOARD IS SEATED CORRECTLY.
BAD COMMAND OR FILENAME	COMMAND FILE COULD BE CORRUPT OR MISSING, IN WRONG PATH OR TYPED IN WRONG.	• CHECK YOUR CONFIG.SYS AND AUTOEXEC.BAT FILES FOR MISSING COMMANDS, INCORRECT PATHS OR TYPO'S.
CHECKSUM ERROR	THE CMOS RAM COULD BE CORRUPT.	• RESTORE SETTINGS IN CMOS TO DEFAULT SETTINGS.
DATA ERROR OR SECTOR NOT FOUND	SYSTEM CAN NOT READ FROM THE HARD DISK OR FLOPPY.	• NEED TO RUN CHKDISK ON THE SUSPECTED DISK.
GATE A20 FAILED MEMORY ERROR	MEMORY FAILED.	• CHECK TO SEE IF THE MEMORY CARDS ARE SEATED CORRECTLY. • INSTALL NEW MEMORY CARDS.

BEEP CODE OR ERROR MESSAGE	DESCRIPTION	WHAT TO DO
HARD DISK FAILURE	HARD DRIVE FAILED.	• CHECK CMOS TO SEE IF THE SETTING FOR THE HARD DRIVE ARE CORRECT. • MAKE SURE THE SETTINGS ON THE HARD DRIVE ARE CORRECT (MASTER OR SLAVE) • REPLACE HARD DRIVE.

ORIGINAL IBM BEEP CODES

BEEPS	DESCRIPTION	WHAT TO DO
1 SHORT	NORMAL POST	SYSTEM IS NORMAL
2 SHORT	POST ERROR	THE ERROR CODE IS SHOWN ON SCREEN.
NO BEEP	POWER SUPPLY OR SYSTEM BOARD PROBLEM.	DISCONNECTED CPU OR DISCONNECTED SPEAKER.
CONTINUOUS BEEP	POWER SUPPLY, SYSTEM BOARD OR KEYBOARD PROBLEM.	TRY SWAPPING OUT THE KEYBOARD WITH A KNOWN GOOD ONE FIRST, THEN IF THAT DOESN'T WORK TRY SWAPPING THE POWER SUPPLY AND FINALLY THE SYSTEM BOARD.

BEEPS	DESCRIPTION	WHAT TO DO
REPEATING SHORT BEEPS	POWER SUPPLY, KEYBOARD OR SYSTEM PROBLEM.	TRY SWAPPING OUT THE KEYBOARD WITH A KNOWN GOOD ONE FIRST, THEN IF THAT DOESN'T WORK TRY SWAPPING THE POWER SUPPLY AND FINALLY THE SYSTEM BOARD.
1 LONG & 1 SHORT BEEP	SYSTEM BOARD PROBLEM.	NEW SYSTEM BOARD.
1 LONG & 2 SHORT BEEPS	DISPLAY ADAPTER.	DISPLAY ADAPTER PROBLEM MDA, CGA
1 LONG & 3 SHORT BEEPS	ENHANCED GRAPHICS ADAPTER (EGA).	PROBLEM WITH THE GRAPHICS ADAPTER. SWAP OUT WITH A KNOWN GOOD ONE.
3 LONG BEEPS	3270 KEYBOARD CARD.	NEEDS REPLACED.

PHOENIX BIOS BEEP & POST CODES

BEEPS	POST CODE	WHAT TO DO
1-1-1-3	02	CHECK THAT ITS IN REAL MODE.
1-1-2-1	04	CHECK THE CPU TYPE.
1-1-2-3	06	SYSTEM HARDWARE NEEDS INITIALIZE.
1-1-3-1	08	CHECK TO SEE IF THE CHIP-SET REGISTERS HAVE THE SAME VALUES AS THE POST VALUES.
1-1-3-2	09	SET THE POST FLAG.
1-1-3-3	0A	INITIALIZE THE CPU REGIS-TERS.
1-1-4-1	0C	CHANGE TO CACHE TO THE POST VALUES.
1-1-4-3	0E	INITIALIZE THE INPUT/OUTPUT VALUES.

Beeps	Post Code	What to do
1-2-1-1	10	INITIALIZE THE POWER MANAGEMENT VALUES.
1-2-1-2	11	CHANGE THE VALUE OF THE ALTERNATE REGISTER WITH THE POST VALUES.
1-2-1-3	12	SWITCH JUMPER TO USER-PATCH
1-2-2-1	14	KEYBOARD CONTROLLER NEEDS INITIALIZED.
1-2-2-3	16	BIOS ROM CHECKSUM.
1-2-3-1	18	8254 TIMER INITIALIZATION.
1-2-3-3	1A	8237 DMA CONTROLLER INITIALATION.
1-2-4-1	1C	RESET INTERRUPT CONTROLLER.
1-3-1-1	20	TEST DRAM
1-3-1-3	22	TEST THE 8742 KEYBOARD CONTROLLER.

BEEPS	POST CODE	WHAT TO DO
1-4-1-3	32	TEST THE FREQUENCY FOR THE CPU BUS-CLOCK.
1-4-2-1	34	CMOS RAM READ/WRITE ERROR INDICATES THE CARD NOT SETTED CORRECTLY OR PROBLEM WITH THE ISA BUS.
1-4-2-4	37	CHIPSET NEEDS REINITIALIZED.
1-4-3-1	38	BIOS ROM SHAWDOW SYSTEM.
1-4-3-2	39	NEED TO REINITIALIZE THE CACHE.
1-4-3-3	3A	AUTO SIZE THE CACHE.
1-4-4-1	3C	NEED TO CONFIGURE THE ADVANCED CHIP SET REGISTER
1-4-4-2	3D	NEED TO LOAD THE ALTERNATE REGISTER WITH THE CMOS VALUES.
2-1-1-1	40	SET THE CPU SPEED SETTINGS.

Beeps	Post Code	What to do
2-1-2-4	47	Initialize manager for the PCI in ROMs
2-1-3-1	48	Check CMOS for the video configuration.
2-1-3-2	49	Need to initialize PCI bus and devices.
2-1-3-3	4A	Need to initialize all the video adapters.
2-1-4-1	4C	BIOS ROM shadow video.
2-1-4-3	4E	Displays copy right notice.
2-2-1-1	50	CPU type and speed Display.
2-2-1-3	52	Need to test the keyboard
2-2-2-1	54	If enabled set key click.
2-2-2-3	56	Enable the keyboard

Beeps	Post Code	What to do
2-2-3-1	58	Test the intrrupts for unexpected changes.
2-2-3-3	5A	Displays the prompt.
2-2-4-1	5C	Test the RAM betweem 512kb and 640kb.
2-3-1-1	60	Test the expanded memory.
2-3-1-3	62	Test the extended lines of memory address.
2-3-2-1	64	Switch jump to User-Patch1
2-3-2-3	66	Advanced cache registers needs configured.
2-3-3-1	68	Enable the external and CPU caches.
2-3-3-2	69	Need to initialize the SMI handler.
2-3-3-3	6A	Display the external cache size.
2-3-4-1	6C	Display the shadow message.

BEEPS	POST CODE	WHAT TO DO
2-1-1-3	42	INTERUPT VECTORS NEED INITIALIZED.
2-1-2-1	44	SET THE BIOS INTRRUPTS.
2-1-2-3	46	CHECK THE COPY RIGHT NOTICE FOR ROM.

Beeps	Post Code	What to do
3-2-4-1	9C	Power management needs setup.
3-2-4-3	9E	Hardware interrupts need enabled.
3-3-1-1	A0	Time of day needs set.

Beeps	Post Code	What to do
2-3-4-3	6E	Display the non-disposable segments.
2-4-1-1	70	Display the error messages.
2-4-1-3	72	Need to check for configuration errors.
2-4-2-1	74	Test the real time clock.
2-4-2-3	76	Need to check for keyboard errors.
2-4-4-1	7C	Need to set up the hardware interrupt vectors.
2-4-4-3	7E	If present test the co-processor.
3-1-1-1	80	Disable the on board input/output ports.
3-1-1-3	82	External R5232 port needs installed.
3-1-2-1	84	External parallel ports need installed.
3-1-2-3	86	Onboard input and output ports need to be reinitialized.

BEEPS	POST CODE	WHAT TO DO
3-1-3-1	88	BIOS DATA AREA NEEDS INITIALIZED.
3-1-3-3	8A	EXTENDED BIOS DATA AREA NEEDS INITIALIZED.
3-1-4-1	8C	FLOPPY CONTROLLER NEEDS INITIALIZED.
3-2-1-1	90	HARD DISK CONTROLLER NEEDS INITIALIZED.
3-2-1-2	91	LOCAL BUS HARD DRIVE CONTROLLER NEEDS INITIALIZED.
3-2-1-3	92	SWITCH JUMP TO USER-PATCH2.
3-2-2-1	94	A20 ADDRESS LINE NEEDS DISABLED.
3-2-2-3	96	ES SEGMENT REGISTER NEEDS CLEARED.

FILE
EXTENSIONS

BELOW IS A LIST OF FILE
EXTENSIONS GATHERED OVER THE YEARS.
ALONG WITH THE EXTENSION NAME IS A
BRIEF DISCRIPTION OF THE FILE.

EXTENSION	DESCRIPTION
	A EXTENTIONS
A	OBJECT CODE LIBRARY
A5W	AUTHORWARE WINDOWS FILE (UNPACK AGED)
AA	AUDIBLE AUDIO FILE (DOWNLOADABLE AUDIO BOOKS)
ABF	ADOBE BINARY SCREEN FONT
ACA	PROJECT MANAGER WORKBENCH FILE
ADD	OS/2 ADAPTER DRIVER FILE USED IN BOOT PROCESS
ADN	LOTUS 1-2-3 ADD IN FILE
ADX	LOTUS APPROACH DBASE INDEX
AL	ADOBE ILLUSTRATOR DRAWING
AIM	AOL INSTANT MESSENGER LAUNCH FILE
APC	LOTUS 1-2-3 PRINTER DRIVER
API	ADOBE ACROBAT PLUG-IN FILE

EXTENSION	DESCRIPTION
APS	MICROSOFT VISUAL C++ FILE
APX	BORLAND C++ APPEXPERT DATABASE
ART	CLIP ART
ASD	LOTUS 1-2-3 SCREEN DRIVER
ASF	MICROSOFT ADVANCED STREAMING FORMAT
ASH	TASM 3.0 ASSEMBLY LANGUAGE HEADER
ASI	BORLAND C++ / TURBO C ASSEMBLER INCLUDE FILE
ASM	PRO / E ASSEMBLY FILE
ASM	ASSEMBLER LANGUAGE SOURCE FILE
ASP	ACTIVE SERVER PAGE (HTML file containing a MS server-Processed Script)
ASX	VIDEO FILE
ATM	ADOBE TYPE MANAGER data / info FILE
AVG	AVG VIRUS INFORMATION DATABASE

EXTENSION	DESCRIPTION
AVI	MICROSOFT AUDIO VIDEO INTERLEAVED WINDOWS MOVIE FILE
AWE	ACROBAT BOOKMARK XML FILE
AWK	AWK SCRIPT / PROGRAM
AWM	ANIMATION WORKS MOVIE
AXL	ArcIMS XML PROJECT FILE
	B EXTENSTIONS
B	BASIC LANGUAGE SOURCE FILE
BAS	BASIC SOURCE FILE
BAT	BATCH FILE
BBM	DELUXE PAINT BITMAP IMAGE
BCP	BORLAND C++ MAKEFILE
BCW	BORLAND C++ 4.5 ENVIRONMENT SETTINGS FILE

EXTENSION	DESCRIPTION
BDF	ADOBE FONT FILE
BGI	BORLAND GRAPHICS INTERFACE DRIVER
BHF	pcANYWHERE HOST FILE
BI	BINARY FILE
BIB	DATABASE
BIN	BINARY FILE
BIO	OS/2 BIOS FILE
BMP	OS/2 OR WINDOWS BITMAP FILE
BOOK	ADOBE FRAMEMAKER BOOK
BOX	LOTUS NOTE FILE

C EXTENSIONS

CAB	MICROSOFT CABINET FILE
CAC	EXECUTABLE FILE FOR DBASE IV

EXTENSION	DESCRIPTION
CACHE	A shared cache file
CAL	Data file for Calendar schedule
CAT	A DBase catalog file
CBL	Cobol source code
CBT	Computer based training file
CC	C++ source code file
CDFS	Compact disk filing system
CDM	Custom data module for Visual DBase
CDR	Data file for the raw audio cd
CEF	Cruzer usb flash drive encrypted files
CFG	Configuration file
CFM	ColdFusion template file
CHF	PCanywhere remote control file

EXTENSION	DESCRIPTION
CHK	WIDOWS DEFRAGMENTER OR SCANDISK FILES
CLASS	JAVA CLASS FILE
CLP	WINDOWS CLIPBOARD FILE
CLS	C++ CLASS FILE
CLS	CLASS FILE FOR VISUAL BASIC
CLX	ADOBE
CMA	PLAIN TEXT FORMATE DBASE FILE
CMD	DOS CP/M COMMAND-LINE FILE
CMYK	RAW CYAN, YELLOW, MAGENTA AND BLACK BYTES
CNT	SYSTEM CONTENT FILES FOR HELP INDEXES
COB	SOURCE CODE FOR COBOL PROGRAMMING LANGUAGE
COD	FORTRAN COMPILED PROGRAMMING CODE
COD	TEMPLATE SOURCE FILE FOR DBASE APPLICATION GENERATOR

EXTENSION	DESCRIPTION
COD	Microsoft C compiler with assembly output
COM	Command file
CPM	Turbo Pascal programming language DOS file
CPP	C++ programming language source code
CRT	Certificate

D EXTENSIONS

EXTENSION	DESCRIPTION
DAT	Data file
DB	Microsoft access database
DBK	Database dbase backup
DBO	DBase iv compiled program file
DOC	MS Word document
DV	Digital video file

EXTENSION	DESCRIPTION
DVF	CAMCORDER GRAPHICS FILE
DWF	VECTOR GRAPHIC'S FILE

E EXTENSIONS

EXTENSION	DESCRIPTION
EXE	EXECUTABLE FILE
EXT	EXTENSION FILE

F EXTENSIONS

EXTENSION	DESCRIPTION
FLV	MACROMEDIA FLASH VIDEO
FM	ADOBE FRAMEMAKER DOCUMENT
FTP	FILE TRANSFER PROTOCOL

EXTENSION	DESCRIPTION
H EXTENSIONS	
H	C PROGRAM HEADER FILE
H++	C++ HEADER FILE
HH	C++ HEADER FILE
HIV	REGISTRY HIVE FOR WINDOWS NT
HST	HISTORY FILE
HT	HYPER TERMINAL
HTM	HTML MARKUP LANGUAGE
HTML	HTML MARKUP LANGUAGE
I EXTENSIONS	
INF	INFORMATION FILE
INI	SETUP FILE

EXTENSION	DESCRIPTION
INI	Initialization file
INS	Install script from InstallShield
INT	Excutable code produced when program is checked for syntex errors.
ISO	CD-Rom files with the iso 9660 standard

J EXTENSIONS

EXTENSION	DESCRIPTION
JAR	Java archive of compressed files containing a Java application package and related files.
JAVA	Java source code
JCP	Java process file
JFIF	JPEG image file
JIF	JPEG image file
JPE	JPEG imange file
JPEG	Compressed bitmap file

EXTENSION	DESCRIPTION
JPG	JPEG bitmap
JPG2	Bitmap file
JS	Javascript source code file
JTF	JPEG bitmap
JTK	Java tool-kit file by Sun Microsystems

K EXTENSIONS

KEY	Security file

M EXTENSIONS

MAK	Make file generic
MAK	Microsoft C++ or Visual Basic file
MAP	Ggeneric map file

EXTENSION	DESCRIPTION
MK	GENERIC MAKE FILE
MKE	MICROSOFT MAKE FILE
MMF	MICROSOFT MAIL FILE
MOV	QUICKTIME WINDOWS MOVIE FILE
MP2	MPEG AUDIO LAYER 2 MIME FILE
MP3	MPEG AUDIO LAYER 3 MIME FILE
MPE	MPEG ANIMATION FILE
MPEG	MPEG ANIMATION FILE
MPG	MPEG ANIMATION FILE

N EXTENSIONS

NT	MICROSOFT WINDOWS NT STARTUP FILES

EXTENSION	DESCRIPTION

O EXTENSIONS

OBJ	OBJECT FILE

P EXTENSIONS

PAS	BORLAND PASCAL SOURCE CODE FILE
PDF	ADOBE ACROBAT PORTABLE DOCUMENT FILE
PNG	ADOBE FIREWORKS FILE BITMAP FILE

Q EXTENSIONS

QRY	MICROSOFT QUERY FILE
QTIF	QUICKTIME IMAGE FILE
QTM	QUICKTIME MOVIE FILE

EXTENSION	DESCRIPTION
	R EXTENSIONS
RAS	Bitmap image
RAW	Bitmap file format
RBF	Rollback file for windows installer
REC	Record file
REF	Generic reference file
REG	Registration file
RGB	Graphics image file from Silicon
	S EXTENSIONS
SCH	Microsoft schedule file
SIG	Signature file

EXTENSION	DESCRIPTION
	T EXTENSIONS
TAR	TAPE ARCHIVE FILE
TAZ	TAR COMPRESSED ASCII ARCHIVE
TBL	OS/2 TABLE OF VALUES
THS	WORDPERFECT THESAURUS DICTIONARY FOR WINDOWS
TIF	TIFF TAG IMAGE BITMAP FILE
TIFF	TIFF TAG IMAGE BITMAP FILE
TMP	MICROSOFT WINDOWS TEMP FILE
TOC	ADOBE FRAMEMAKER TABLE OF CONTENTS FILE
TP	TURBO PASCAL CONFIGURATION FILE

EXTENSION	DESCRIPTION
	V EXTENSIONS
VGA	VGA MONITOR VIDEO GRAPHICS ARRAY DISPLAY
	X EXTENSIONS
XHTML	EXTENSIBLE HYPERTEXT MARKUP LANGUAGE
	Z EXTENSIONS
ZIP	COMPRESSED ARCHIVE FILE